NEWMUSICSHELF

Anthology of New Music

Alto Saxophone, Vol. 1

Alto Saxophone Part

Curated by Alan Theisen

Edited by Dennis Tobenski

NEWMUSICSHELF
www.newmusicshelf.com

NEWMUSICSHELF, INC.

Published in the United States of America
by NewMusicShelf, Inc.
34-29 32nd St., 3rd floor, Astoria, NY 11106
www.newmusicshelf.com

Copyright © 2020 by NewMusicShelf, Inc.

First printing January 2020.

CONTENTS

Written for and commissioned by Alan Jude Theisen

I. Mind

from *Amare*

STEPHANIE ANN BOYD
(2016)

29
p whispering
33
mf
f
37
mf feeling hazy, warm
45
p
53
mf
56
f
61
p sub.

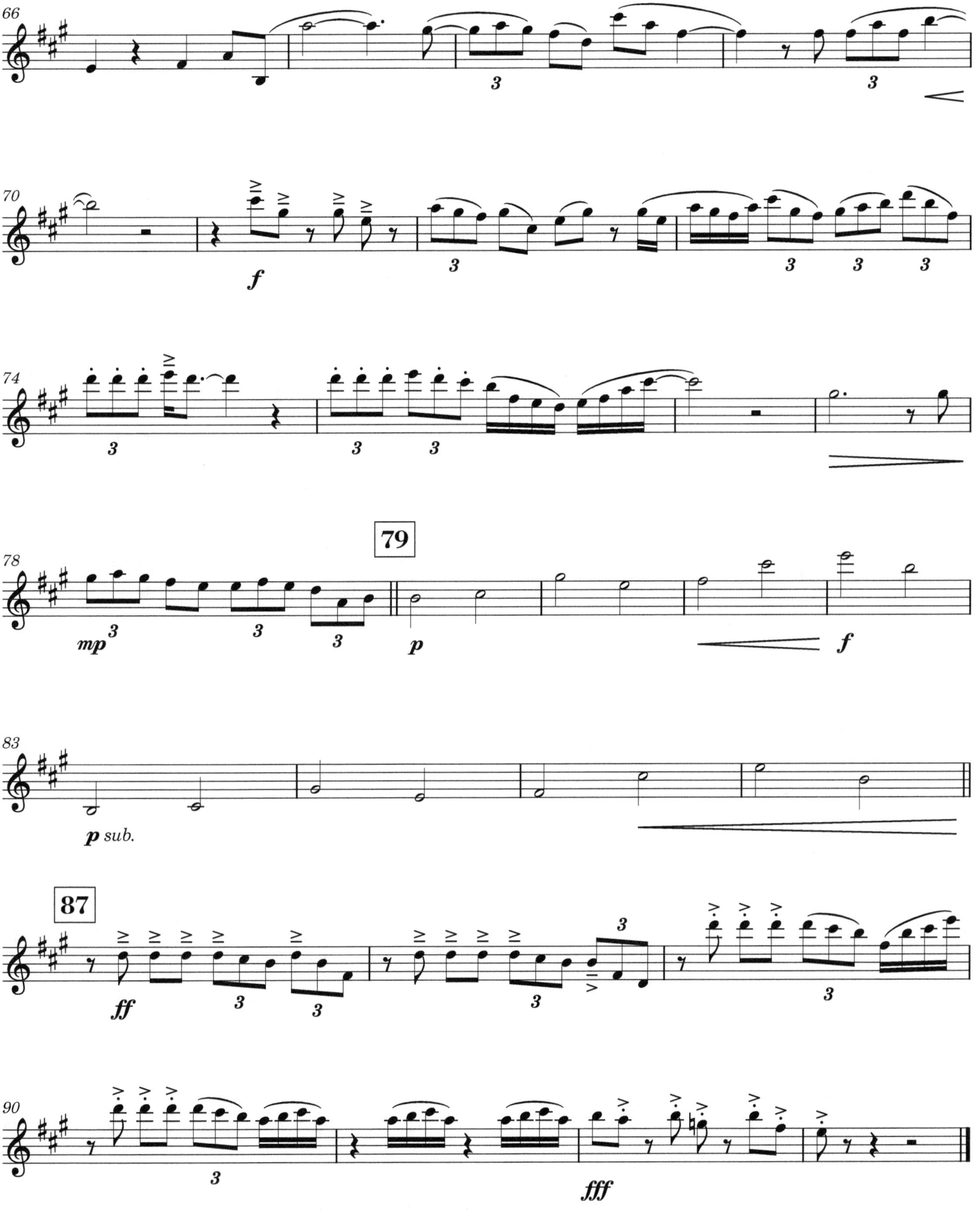
66
70
f
74
78
mp
79
p
f
83
p sub.
87
ff
90
fff

for Jonathan Ahl

An Unperfect Actor

(after Sonnet XXIII)

WES FLINN
(2013)

Moderate (♩ = 82)

mp

6

(♩ = ♩)

mf

9

f

6   6   6   6   6   6

11

accel. . rit. a tempo

15

mf

p

5

18

mf

22
mp
25
(consistent 8th notes throughout)
f
30
34
p
mf
p
mp
37
mp
42
f
46

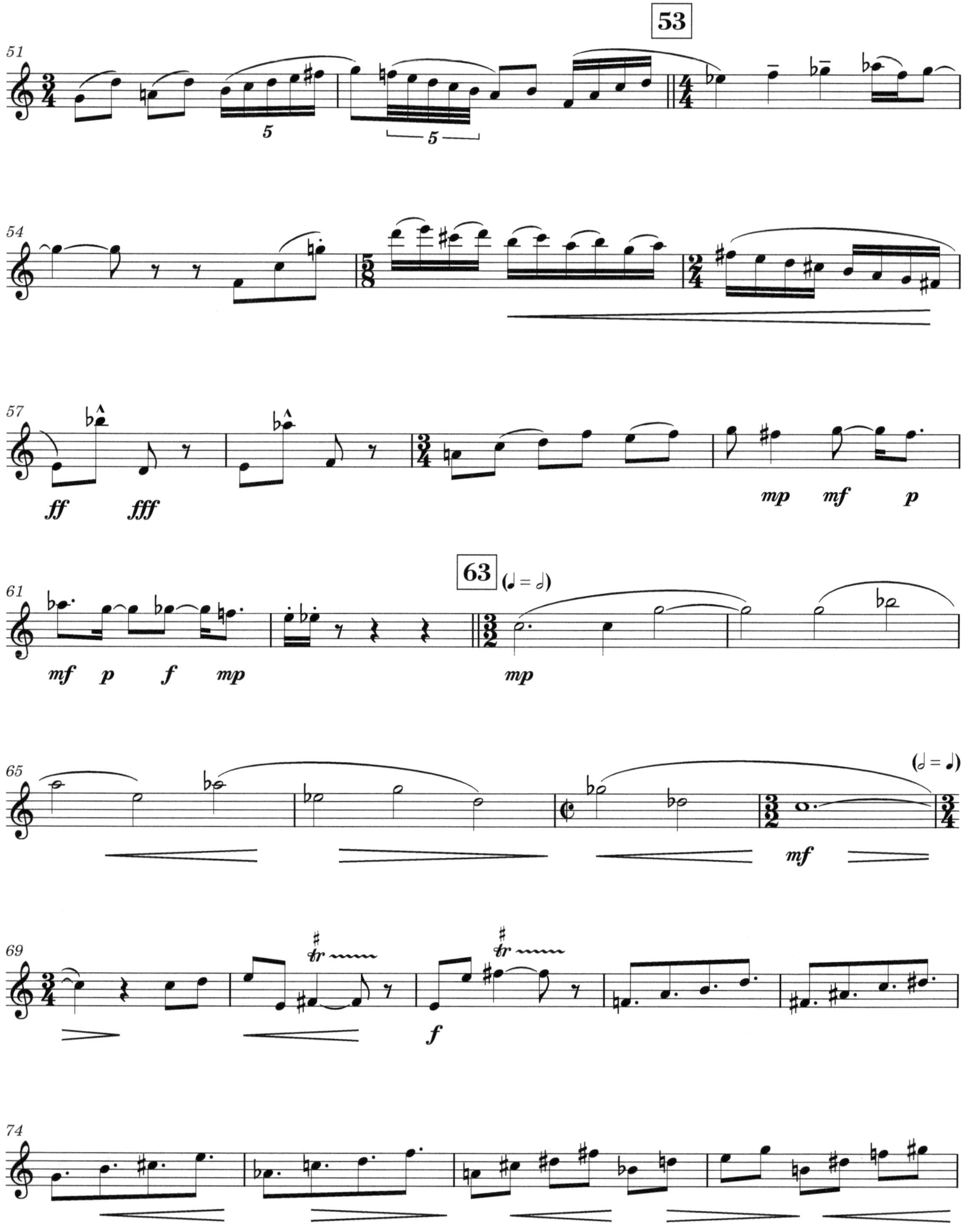
53
63
ff
fff
mp
mf
p
f
tr

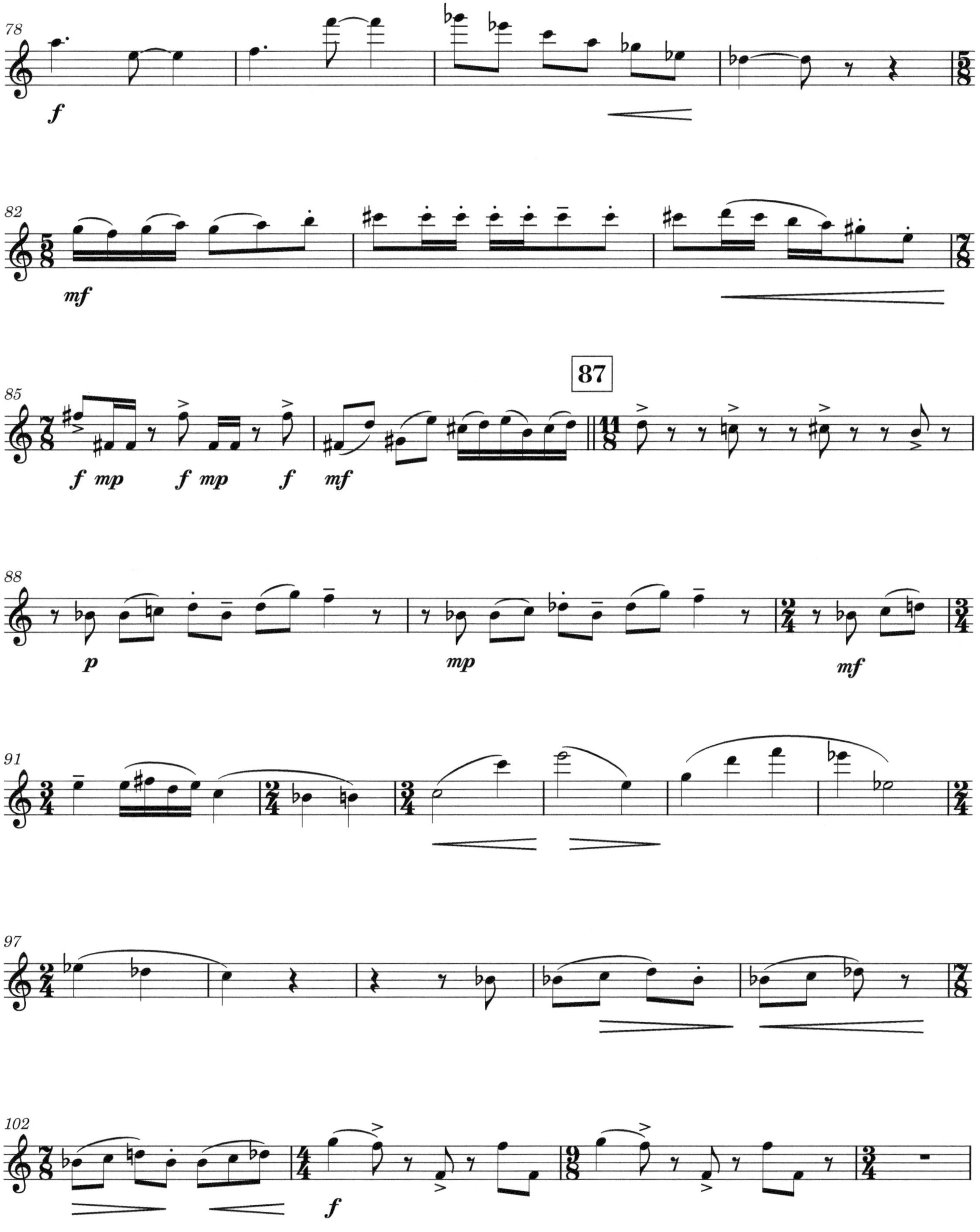
78
f
82
mf
85
87
f mp
f mp
f
mf
88
p
mp
mf
91
97
102
f

106
mf
f
mf
111
f
mf
mf
115
rit. .
ten.
(♩ = 𝅗𝅥)
mp
mf
119
a tempo
mp
f
123
mf
p
mp
128
ten.
(slow to fast to slow)
tr
p
ppp
p
n

This page intentionally left blank to facilitate page turns

for Michael Mortarotti
No. 2: Adagio Espressivo
from *Three Scherzi, Op. 26b*

GEORGE N. GIANOPOULOS
(2013)

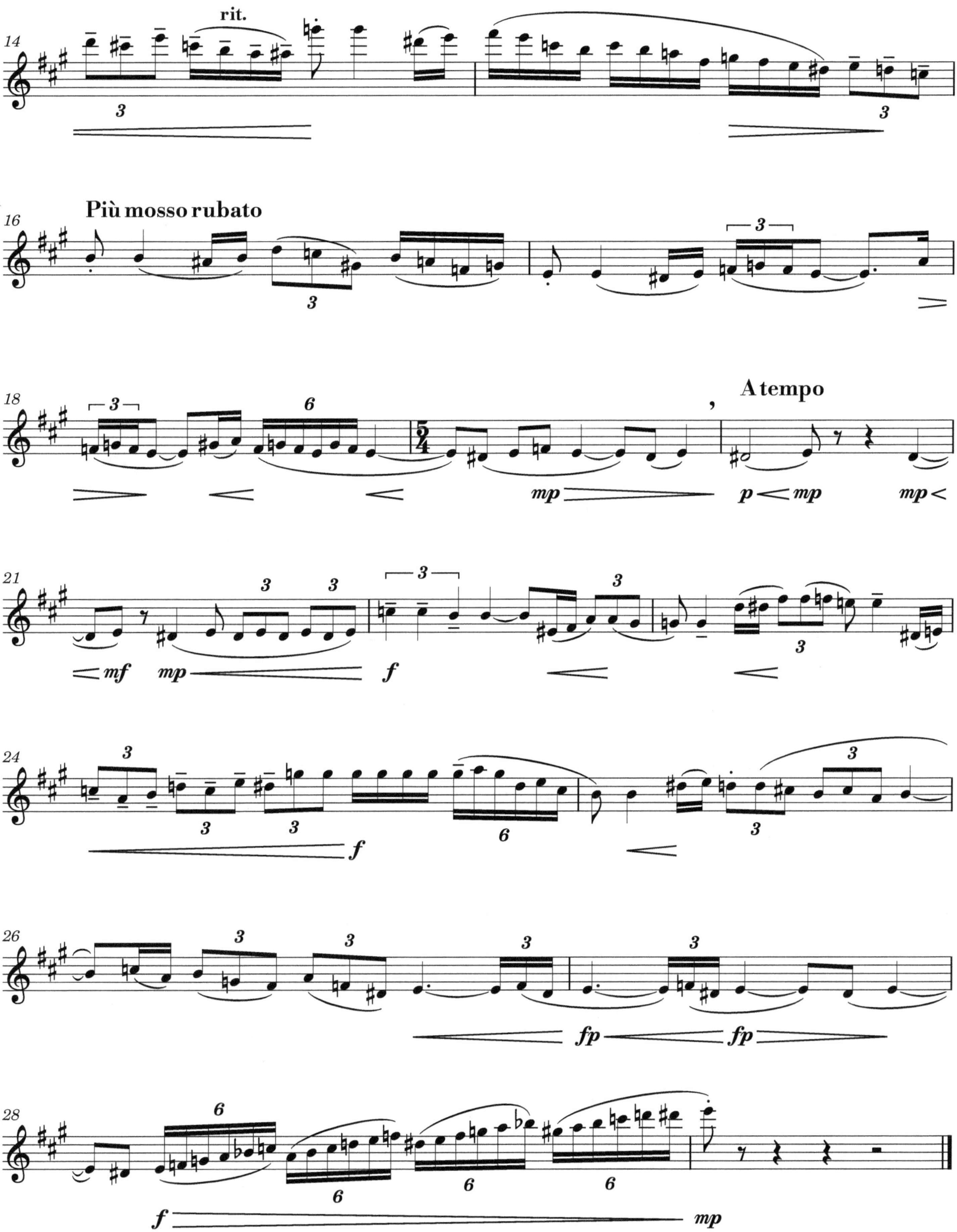
rit.
Più mosso rubato
A tempo
mp
p
mp
mp
mf
mp
f
f
fp
fp
f
mp

dhakira: a middle eastern reflection

Preface

Having been inspired by the calls to prayer in predominantly Muslim cities or cities with public Muslim prayer calls (like northern Nicosia, Akko, and Istanbul), I found myself recording these calls with my cell phone voice recordeer, and listening to the files from time to time. When the singer is talented, the call is immediately transcendental – it interrupts your state of mind and transports you to another place. Perhaps a reverent, spiritual place? A place of calm? Reflection? Meditation? The calls themselves are riddled by silences that demand your attention. It is a silence that simultaneously has tension and does not have tension. It is truly fascinating.

dhakira: a middle eastern reflection is an homage to this Muslim tradition. It is an attempt to create a saxophone version of these calls, while including "every day" sounds within. The word dhakira means memory in Arabic. This piece was written for #RESISTANCE #RESILIENCE, a project by Castle of our Skins, and it is dedicated to its premieresse, Seychelle Dunn-Corbin.

Performance Notes

This work should be performed with your utmost freedom, and a sense of spiritual abandon, within the realm of meditative devotion. Wild rubato is encouraged, and exaggeration is welcome.

This work incorporates a number of techniques outside of standard tone production. While some of the notation is explained in the score, below is a more detailed explanation of certain gestures.

Slap tongue – notes with a flageolet above indicate slap tongue. For notes with *sffz* indications, create an extremely percussive sound. Notes with less dynamic, focus more on the indicated pitch.

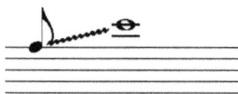

Rip – a wild rip between these two pitches. It can be quick.

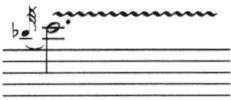

Timbral trill – also called key vibrato or microtonal trill, this gesture is to be executed by trilling between two different fingerings of the same indicated pitch. The second pitch can be microtonally sharp or flat.

Inflection – play the indicated pitch, and during the sustain, play another fingering of the same pitch (it can be microtonally flat or sharp).

air, w/ key clicks
flutter

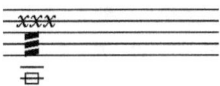

Air, key clicks – all square noteheads indicate an air sound, simply blowing through the instrument to create the sounds of air. The *x x x* above the note indicates to click the keys of the instrument audibly, creating a percussive texture.

Accelerando, ritardando – notes with growing beams are to naturally become faster. Notes with thinning beams are to naturally become slower. **★Note: the number of performed notes in these gestures can be MORE than what is written in the score, but NOT LESS! This is especially true for repeated notes.**

Other notes:

~ While pitch and tone quality is very important, all long sustained pitches in high registers can slightly waver in terms of sharpness or flatness.

~ Gestures/pitches marked *1/2 air* should sound fleeting, but the pitch should still be present.

~ Rhythms can be exaggerated organically.

~ The number of air pitches at the end can increase or decrease by up to 3.

As always, HAVE BIG FUN!!!

for Seychelle

dhakira: a middle eastern reflection

ANTHONY R. GREEN
(2017)

Slow, free, con molto rubato, reverent (♩ = c. 40)

1/2 air

sffz *sffz* *mp* *p whispering* *ff* *f*

mf *pp* *pp* *f* *pp*

fff explosive, interruption

quick lip down

steady, funky

mp *ff* *⌐ 3 ⌐* *< > < > p*

air, w/ key clicks
flutter *sim.*

xxx

p < f *fff* *< > < > < > < > p*

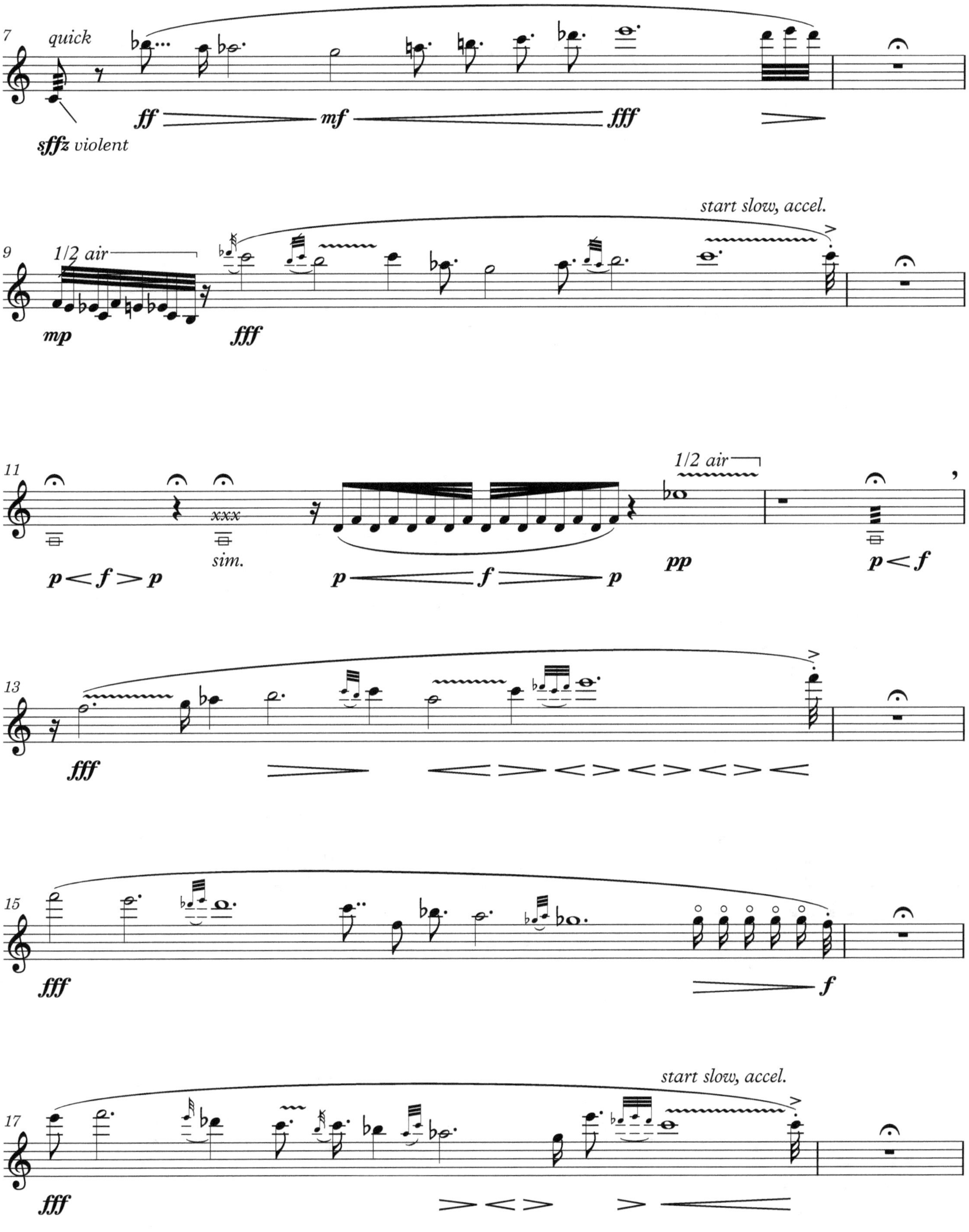
7
quick
ff
mf
fff
sffz violent
start slow, accel.
9
1/2 air
mp
fff
11
1/2 air
xxx
sim.
p < f > p
p
f
p
pp
p < f
13
fff
15
fff
f
start slow, accel.
17
fff

19
1/2 air
xxx
fff
mf > p
p f p
pp
p < mf > p
21
mp fff
mf ff
fff
23
mp fff
sfz
f fff
25
start slow, accel.
mf
fff
mf
fff
27
1/2 air
quick
p
sffz violent fff
mp

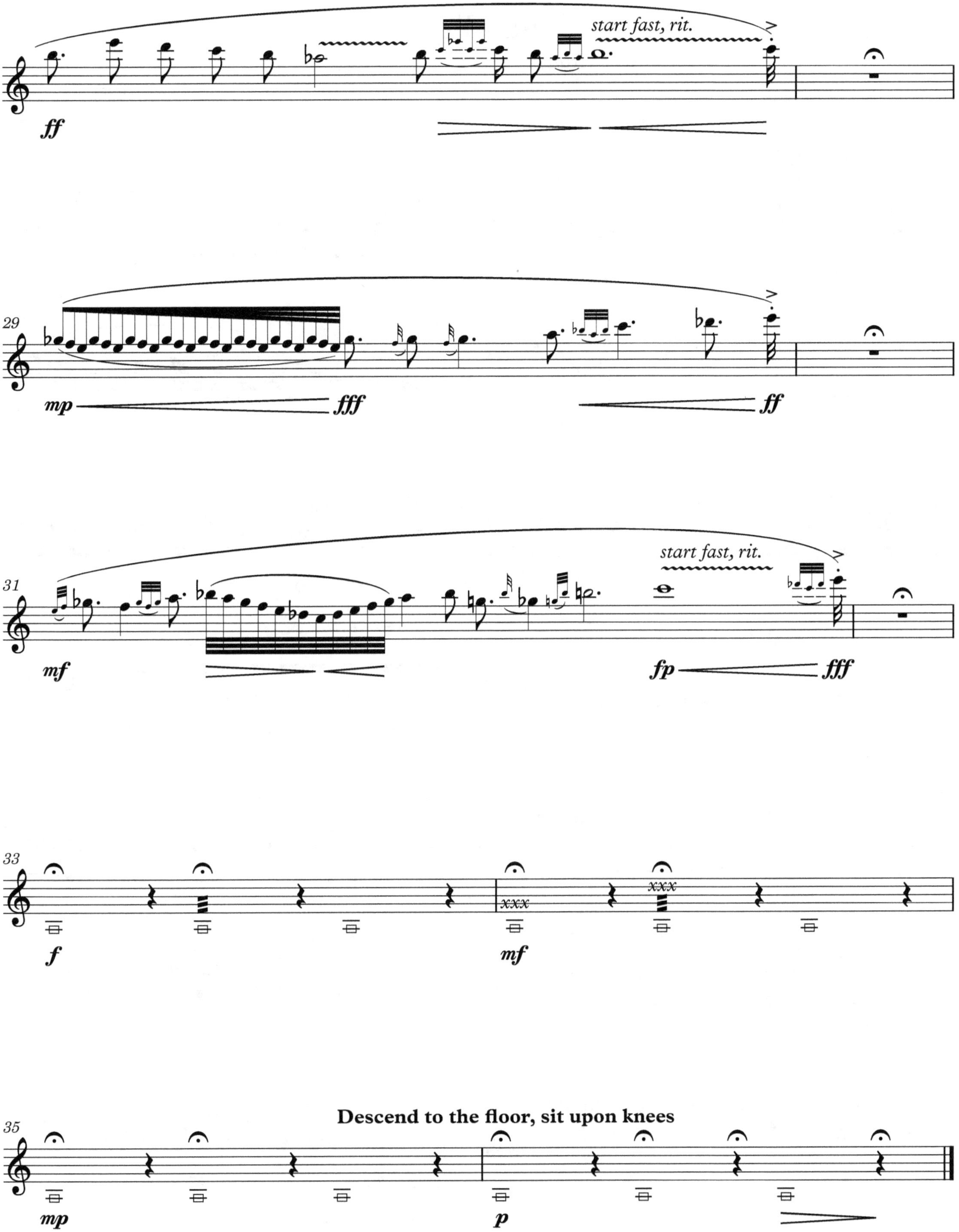
start fast, rit.
ff
29
mp
fff
ff
31
start fast, rit.
mf
fp
fff
33
f
mf
35
Descend to the floor, sit upon knees
mp
p

The Chase

from *Chasing Shadows*

CHIA-YU HSU
(2013)

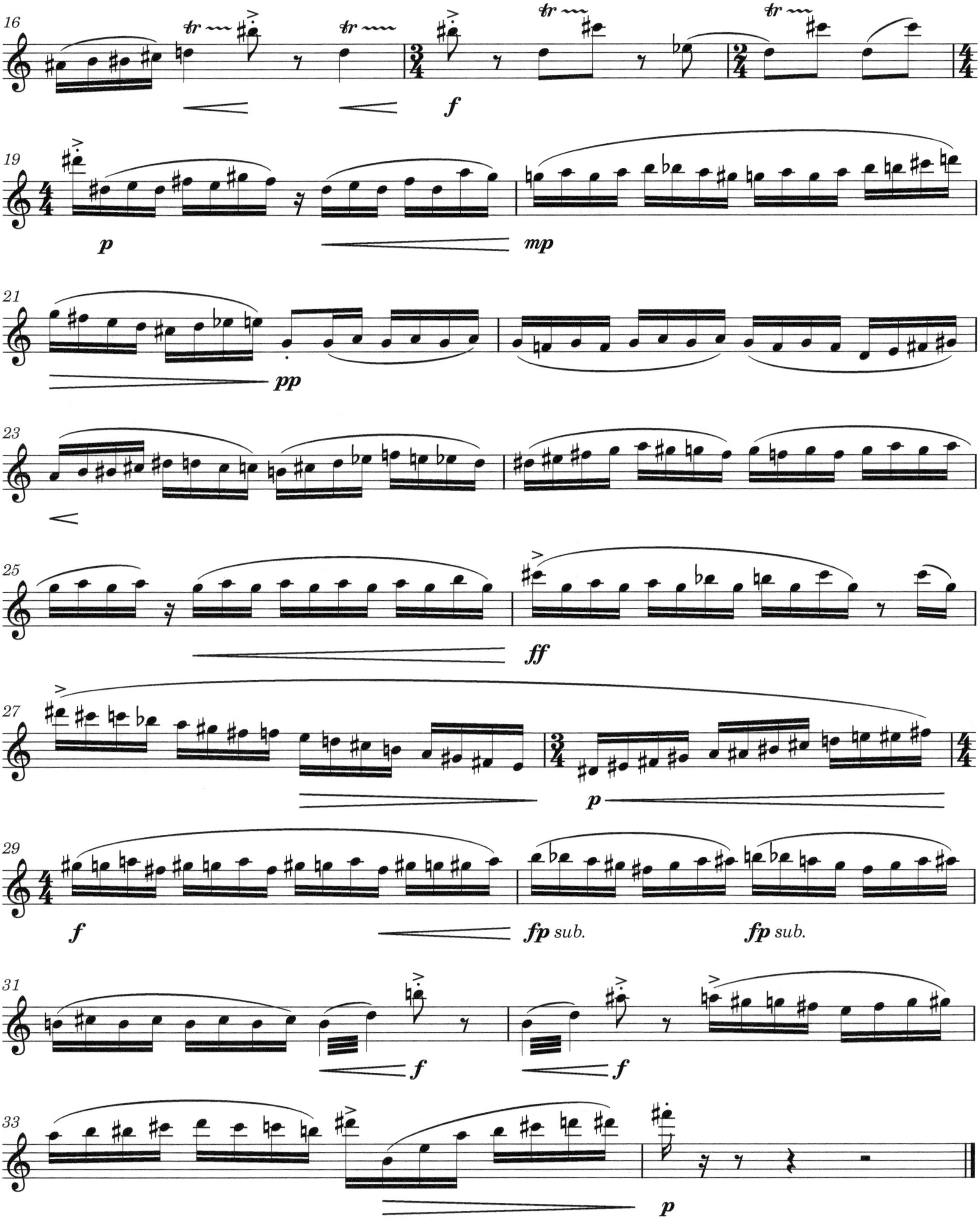
16
tr
tr
f
tr
tr
19
p
mp
21
pp
23
25
ff
27
p
29
f
fp sub.
fp sub.
31
f
f
33
p

for Gary Louie and Kirsten Taylor
Lullaby

LORI LAITMAN
(2000)

Flowing, rubato and legato throughout (♩=120)

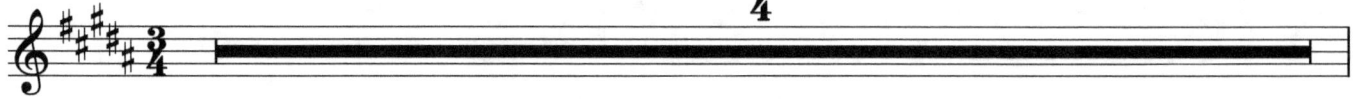

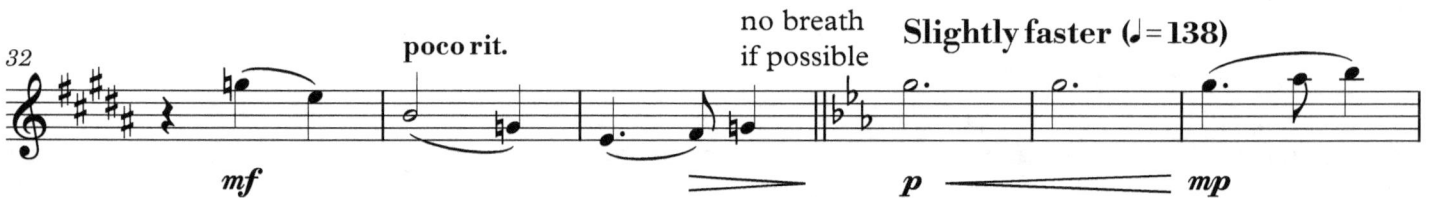

38
p
43
mp
47
mf
f
52
mf
f
mp
mf
poco rit.
2
Tempo I (♩=120)
59
mp
mf
poco rit.
64
mp
p

Bounce
Humoresque for alto saxophone and piano

QUINN MASON
(2016)

30
33
mf
f
mf scherzando
mp
38
2
mf
43
p
48
mf
53
mf
2
mf
p
59
poco
mf
mf
63
p
2

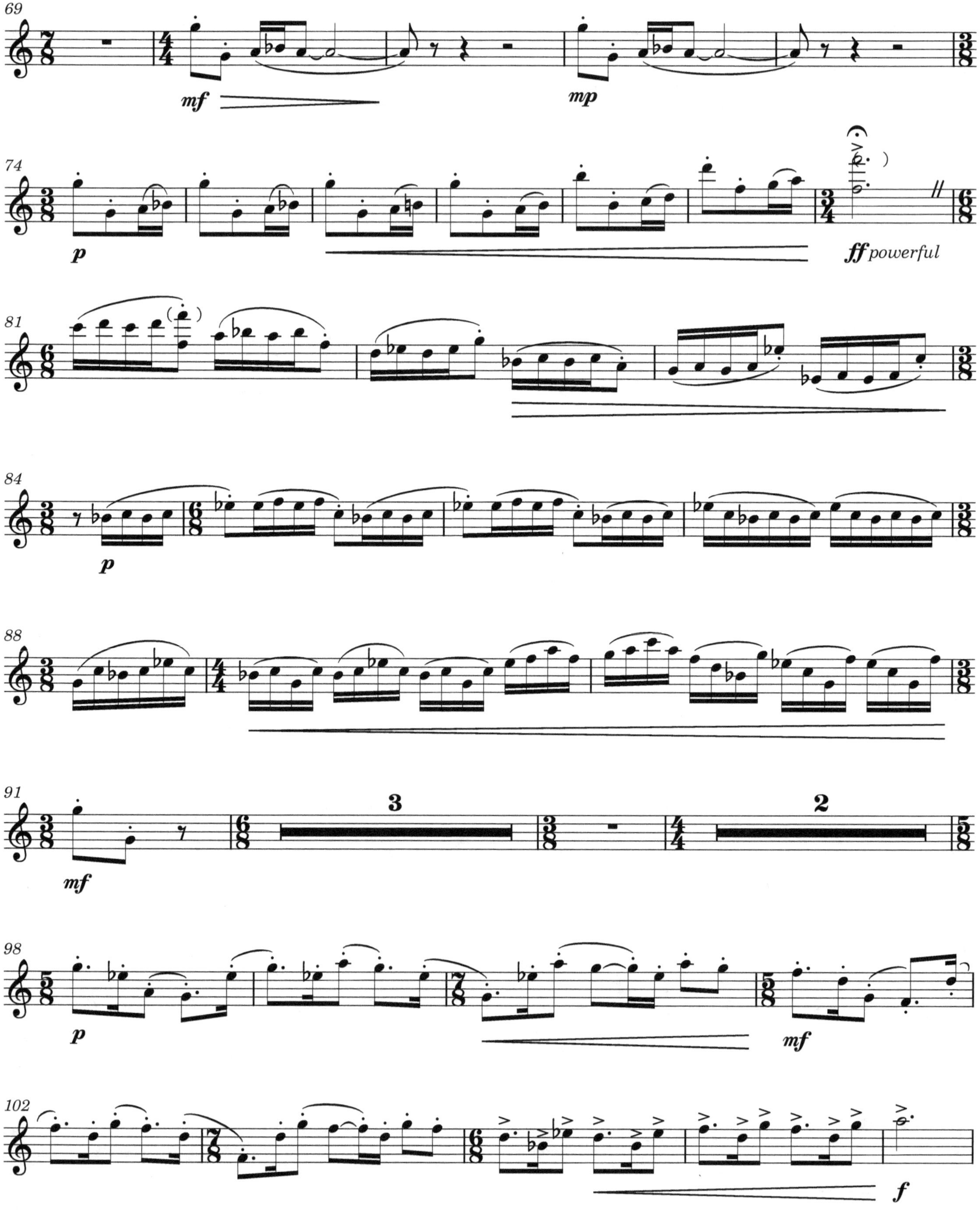
69
mf
mp
74
p
ff powerful
81
84
p
88
91
mf
3
2
98
p
mf
102
f

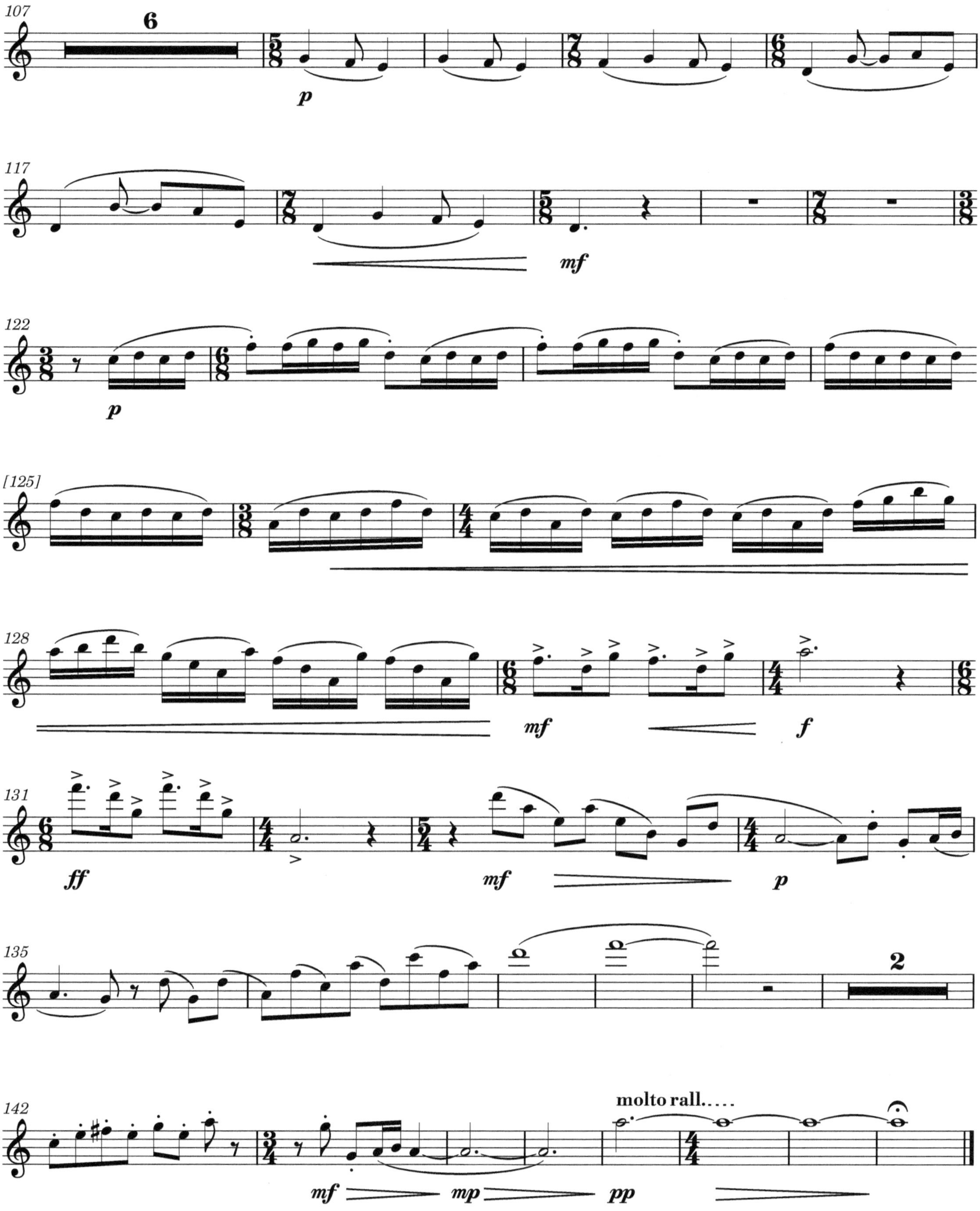
107
6
p
117
mf
122
p
[125]
128
mf
f
131
ff
mf
p
135
2
142
molto rall.....
mf
mp
pp

This page intentionally left blank to facilitate page turns

for Alan Theisen

Fuck Your Factory & Your Attitude

AARON JAY MYERS
(2019)

Funky, edgy, aggressive (♩ = 100)
make pitches "rough" by growling or
humming while playing at your discretion

For the purposes of program listings, the composer has indicated that the title of this piece may be lightly censored (Fuck, F★ck, F★★k, or F★★★) according to the performer's comfort level, or the dictates of the performer's institution.

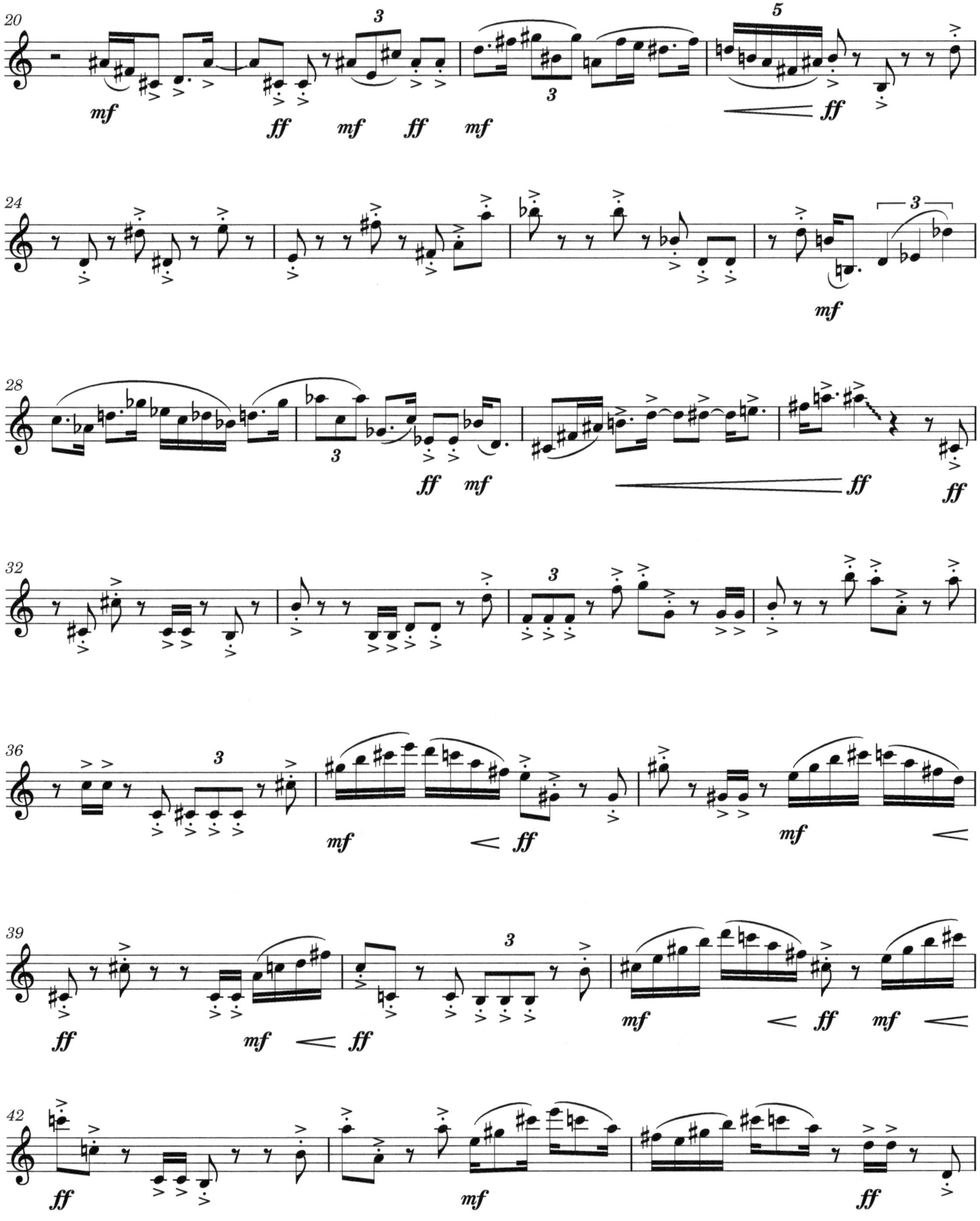

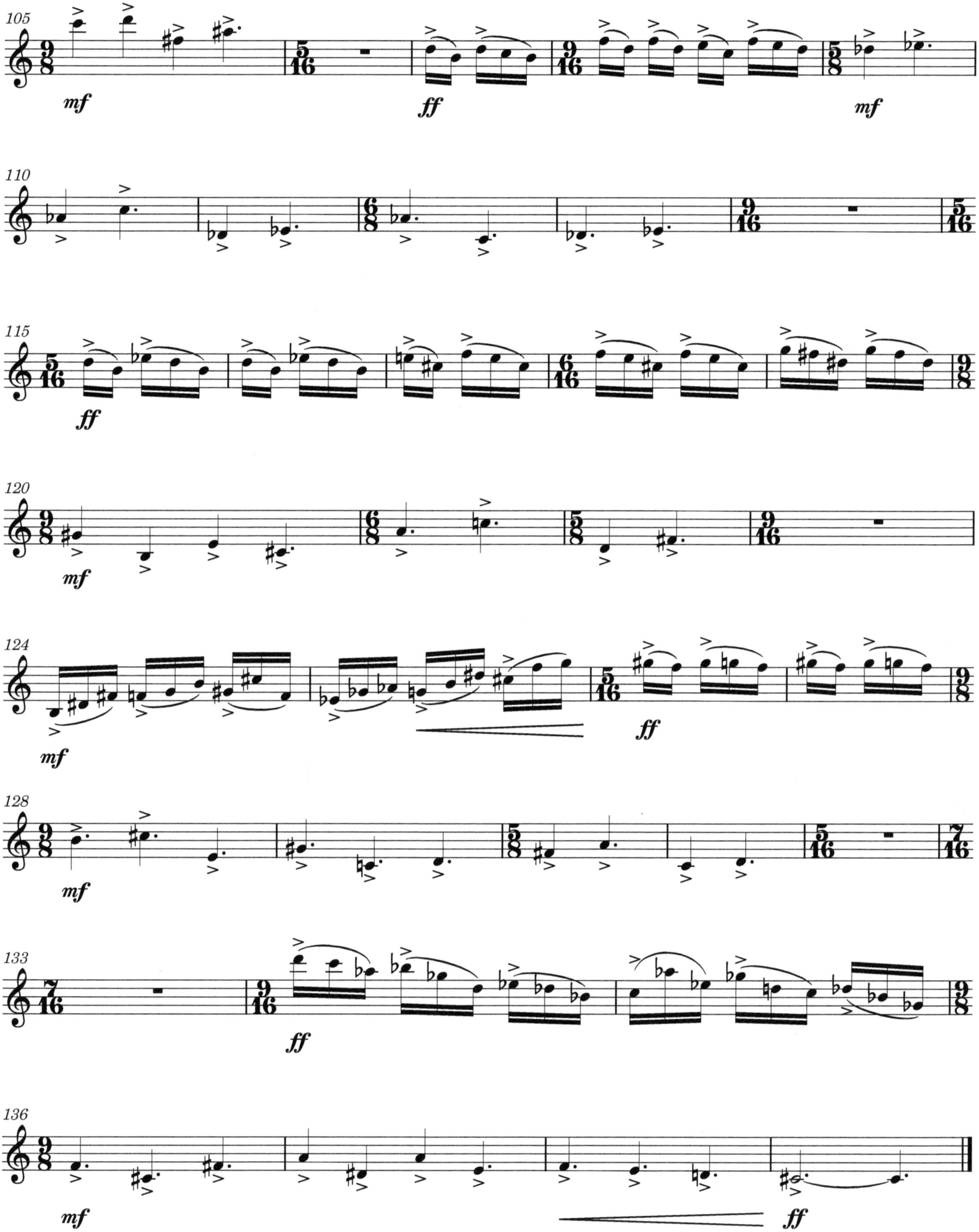
105
mf
ff
mf
110
115
ff
120
mf
124
mf
ff
128
mf
133
ff
136
mf
ff

to Alan Theisen
Absence Wild

GARRETT IAN SHATZER
(2016)

Grave (♩= 54)

Sample ornamentation

9 Ornament freely throughout

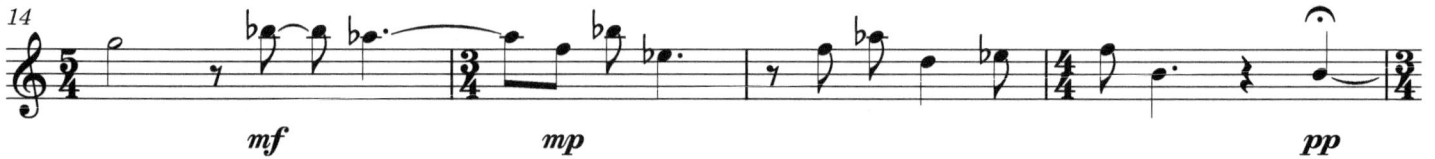

18

poco accel. . . . .

rit.
30 Tempo primo
accel. With motion (♩= 74)
mp
Improvise until m. 45; growing unrest within confines of the piece;
notes written a place to start
mf
f
molto rit.
Silence optional until m. 45
45
Tempo primo

Brief outro lick ending
on anything but I;
release with piano

molto rit.........................

Delicate cadential figure around V

This page intentionally left blank to facilitate page turns

Commissioned by and dedicated to Alan Theisen

Juniper Run

from River Songs

CLARE SHORE
(2016; rev. 2019)

Swing (♩ = c. 152)

(Saxophonist or pianist "counts off"
or pianist raps piano at resonant spot.)

Meno mosso, liberamente (♩ = c. 126)   rit.

♩ = c. 116

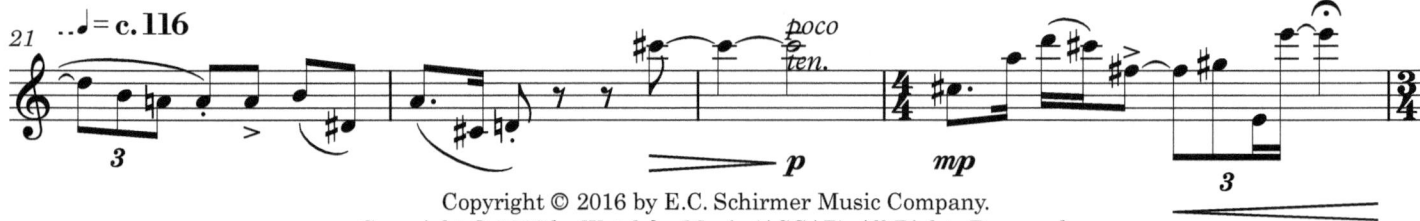

A tempo primo (♩= c. 152)
mf
poco ten.
mp
Meno mosso (♩= c. 116)
breve
f
mp sub.
p

61
f
mp
f
mp
mf
f
mf
f
65
mp
mf
mp
69
♩= c. 116
mp
mf
rit.
Poco meno mosso
73
f
mf
76
a tempo
long bend upward
long bend upward
mp
mf
p
mf
p
81
rit.
Meno mosso (♩= c. 108)
85

89
93
Ossia
fl.
poco rit.
pp
mf
98
♩= c. 92
mp
mf
102
f
Ossia
107
fl.
ff
rit.
accel.
long bend upward
ffp
fff

I. Forcefully
from Sonata for Alto Saxophone and Piano

ALEKSANDER STERNFELD-DUNN
(2009)

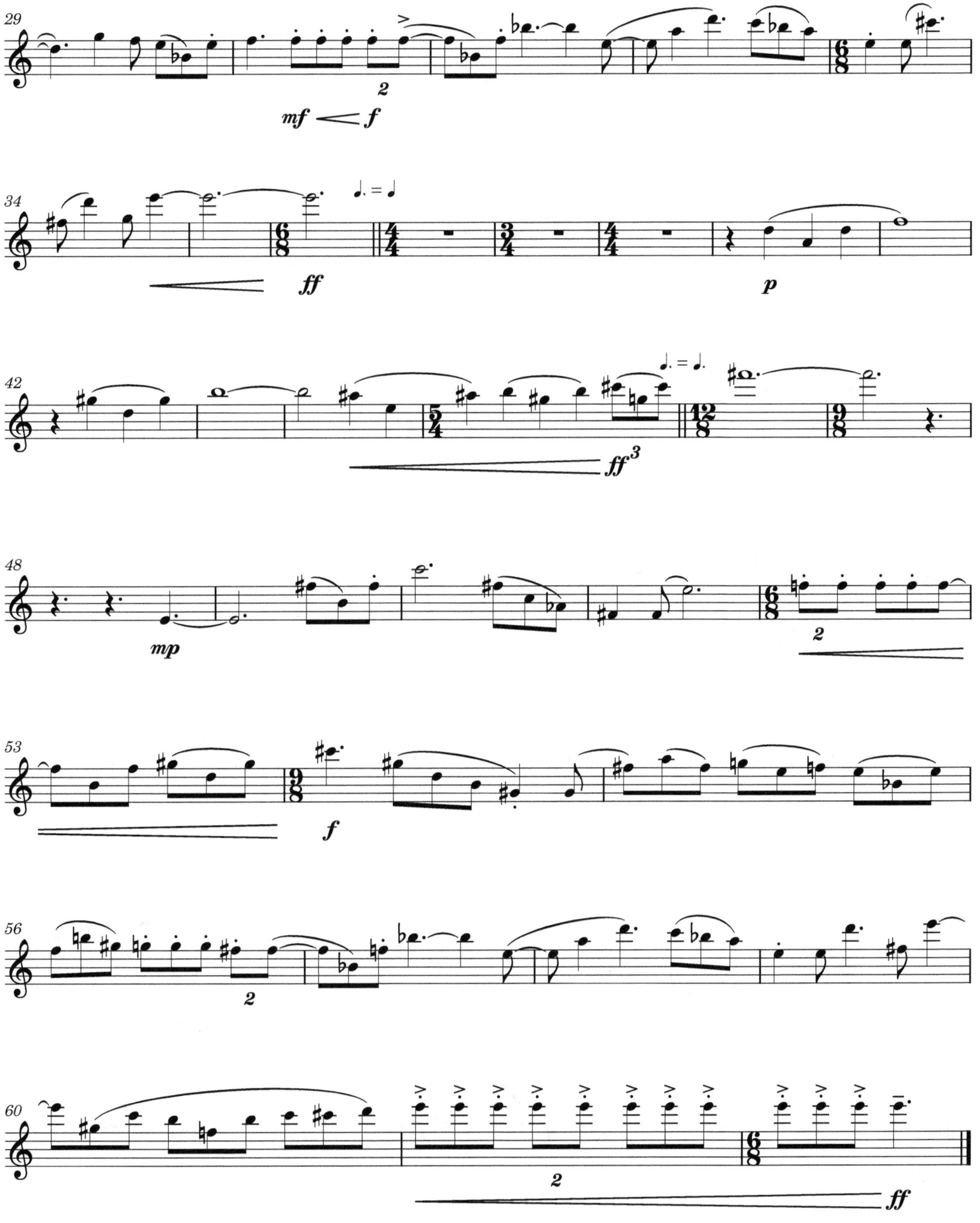

I. Attack

from Saxophone Sonata No. 2

ALAN THEISEN
(2017)

49 **Boogie woogie from hell**

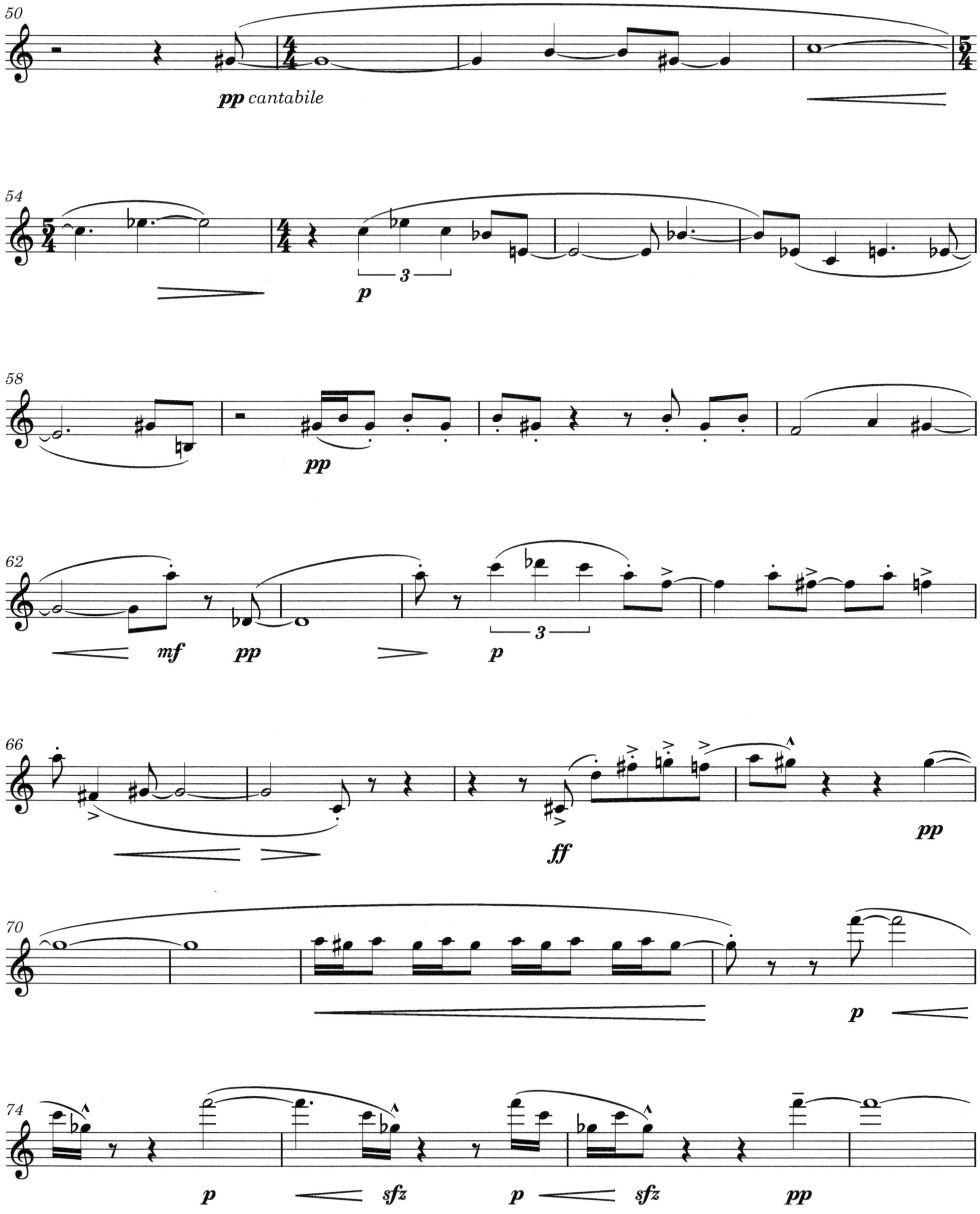
50
pp cantabile
54
p
58
pp
62
mf
pp
p
66
ff
pp
70
p
74
p
sfz
p
sfz
pp

78
81
slap tongue
(or hard, sharp articulation)
p molto rigido
85
f
pp
mp
89
mp
mf
93
mf
f
97
(echo)
pp
100
mf
pp
104
107
ppp
2

try other alternate C# fingerings/manipulations for this passage

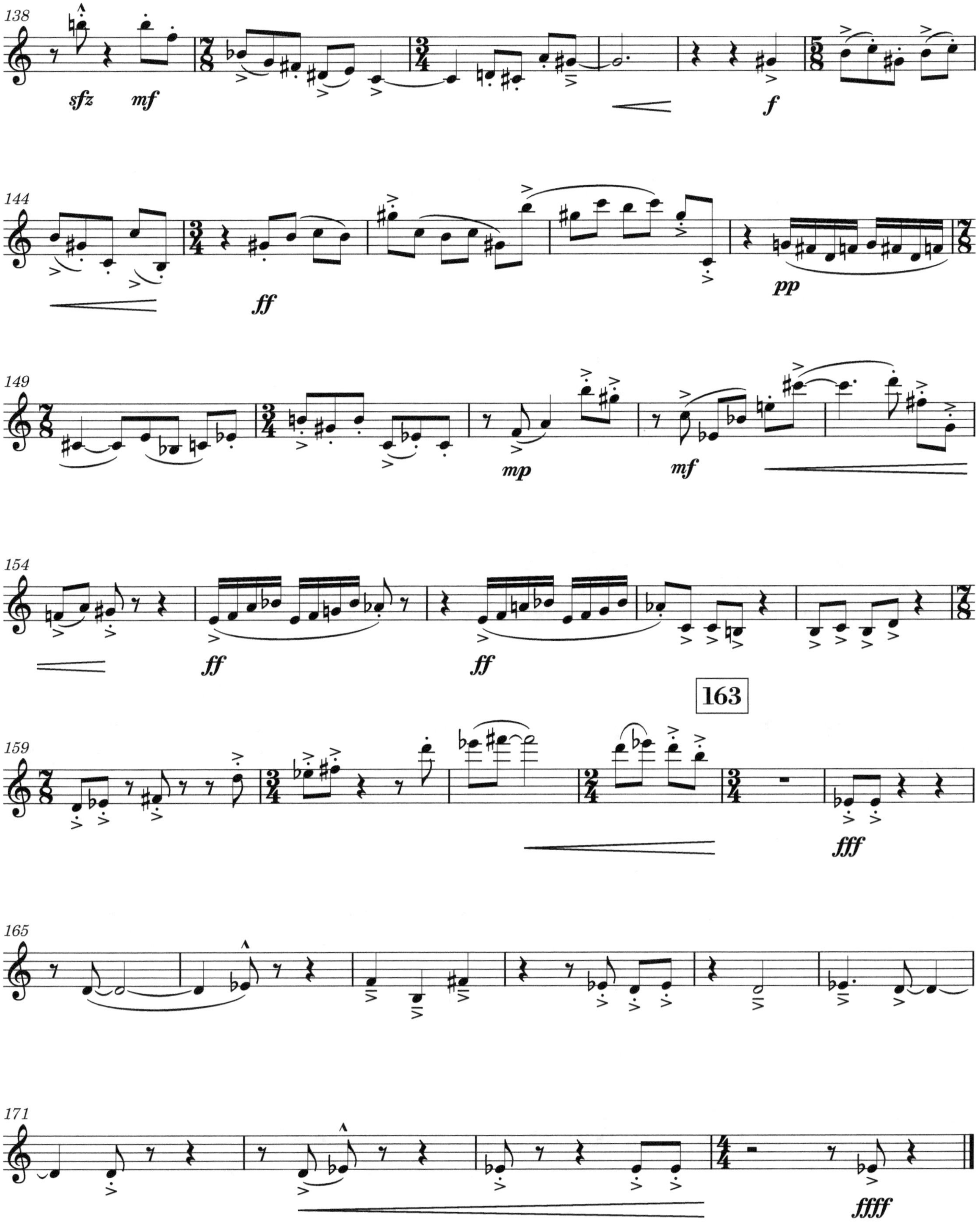
138
sfz mf
f
144
ff
pp
149
mp
mf
154
ff
ff
163
159
fff
165
171
ffff

eyelid

CASSIE WIELAND
(2018)

16
pp
p
pp
19
pp
21
mp
pp
24
pp
mp
pp
27
pp
mp
pp
30
pp
32
mp
pp
pp
35
mp
pp

50

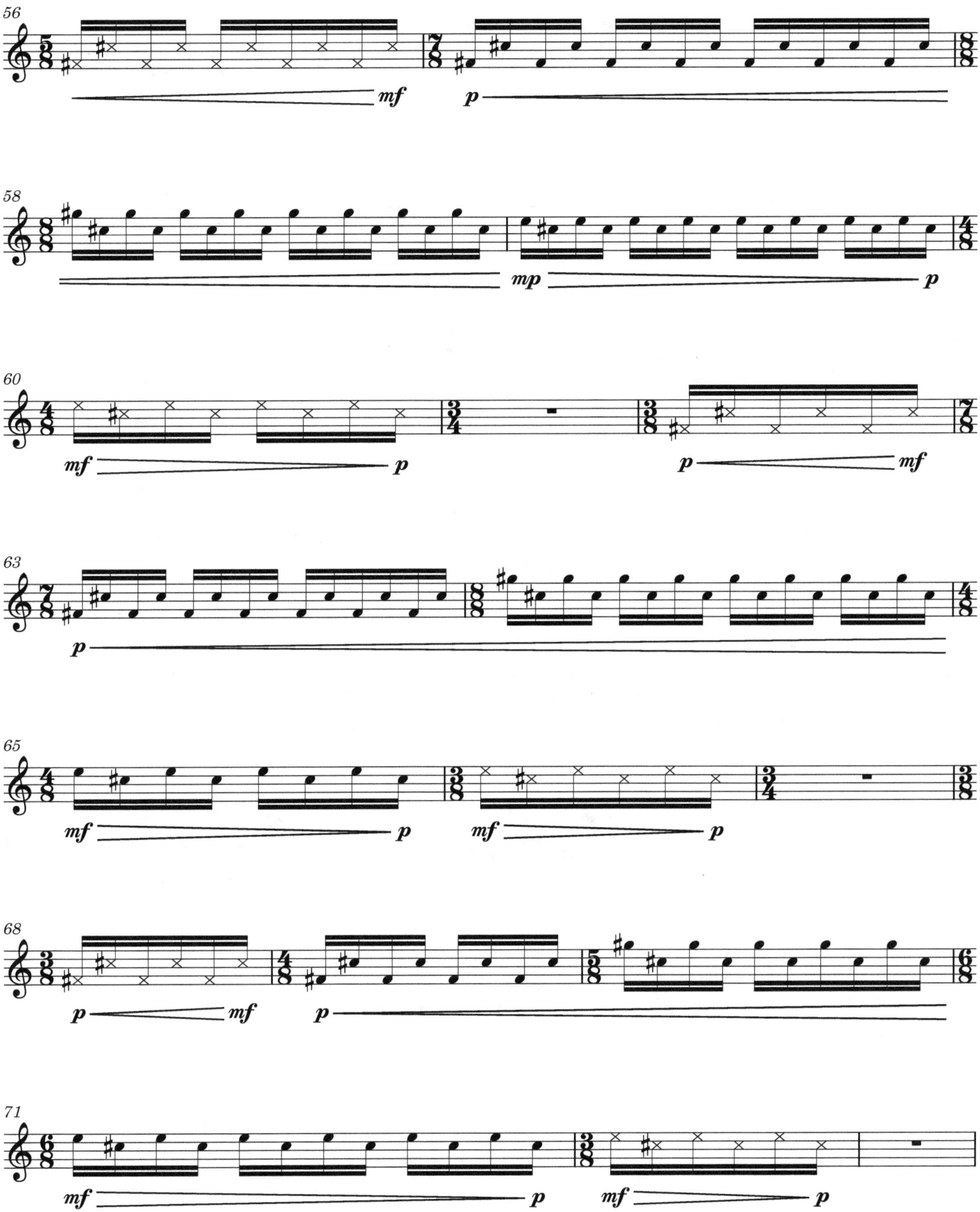
56
mf
p
58
mp
p
60
mf
p
p
mf
63
p
65
mf
p
mf
p
68
p
mf
p
71
mf
p
mf
p

74
p
mf
p
77
mf
p
80
mp
mf
p
84
mp
mf
p
87
breathe when needed
pp
90
p
mp
93
mf
96
f

53

for Dr. Alan Theisen

Move with Brightness of Peace

CHELSEA WILLIAMSON
(2016)

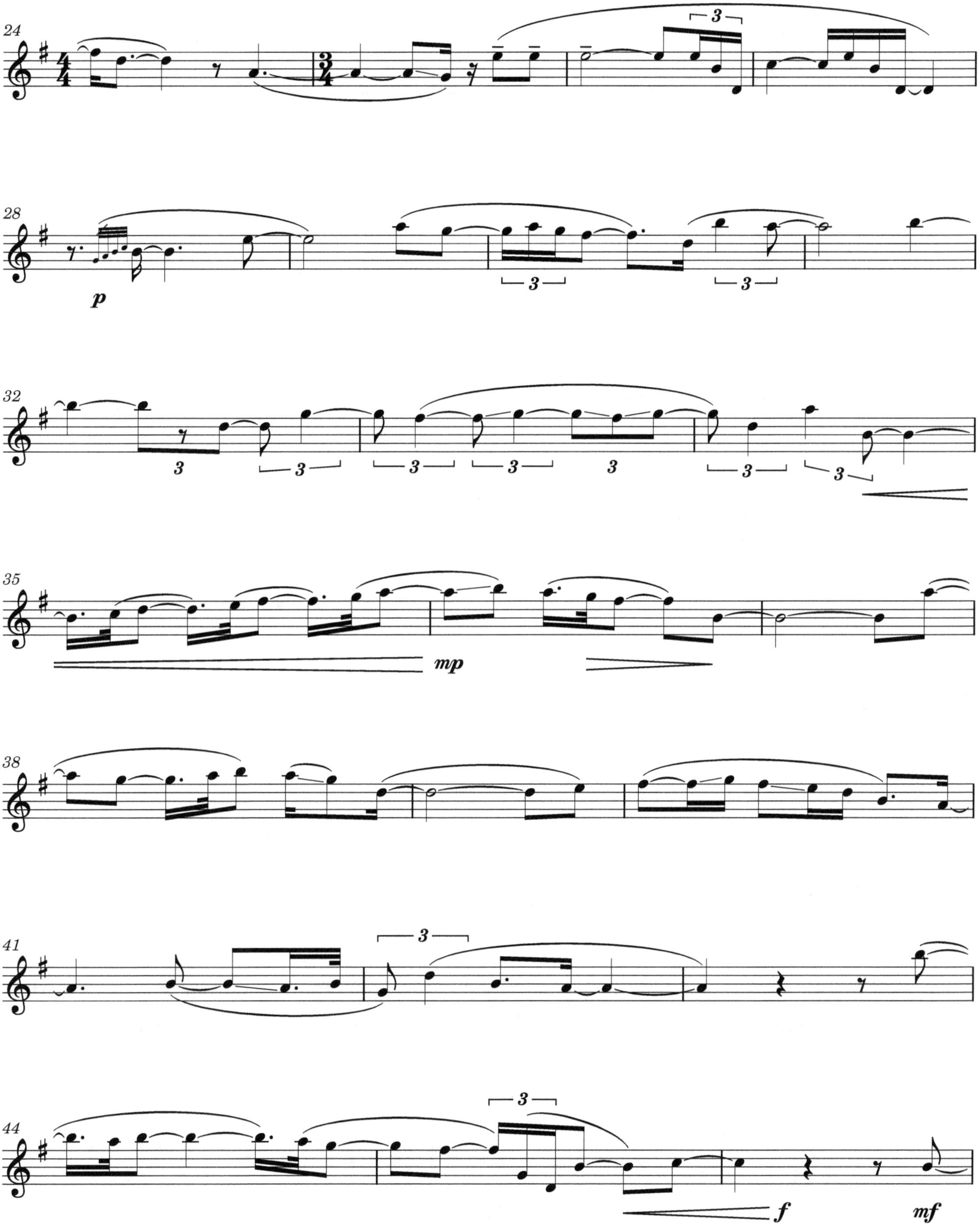
24
28
p
32
35
mp
38
41
44
f
mf

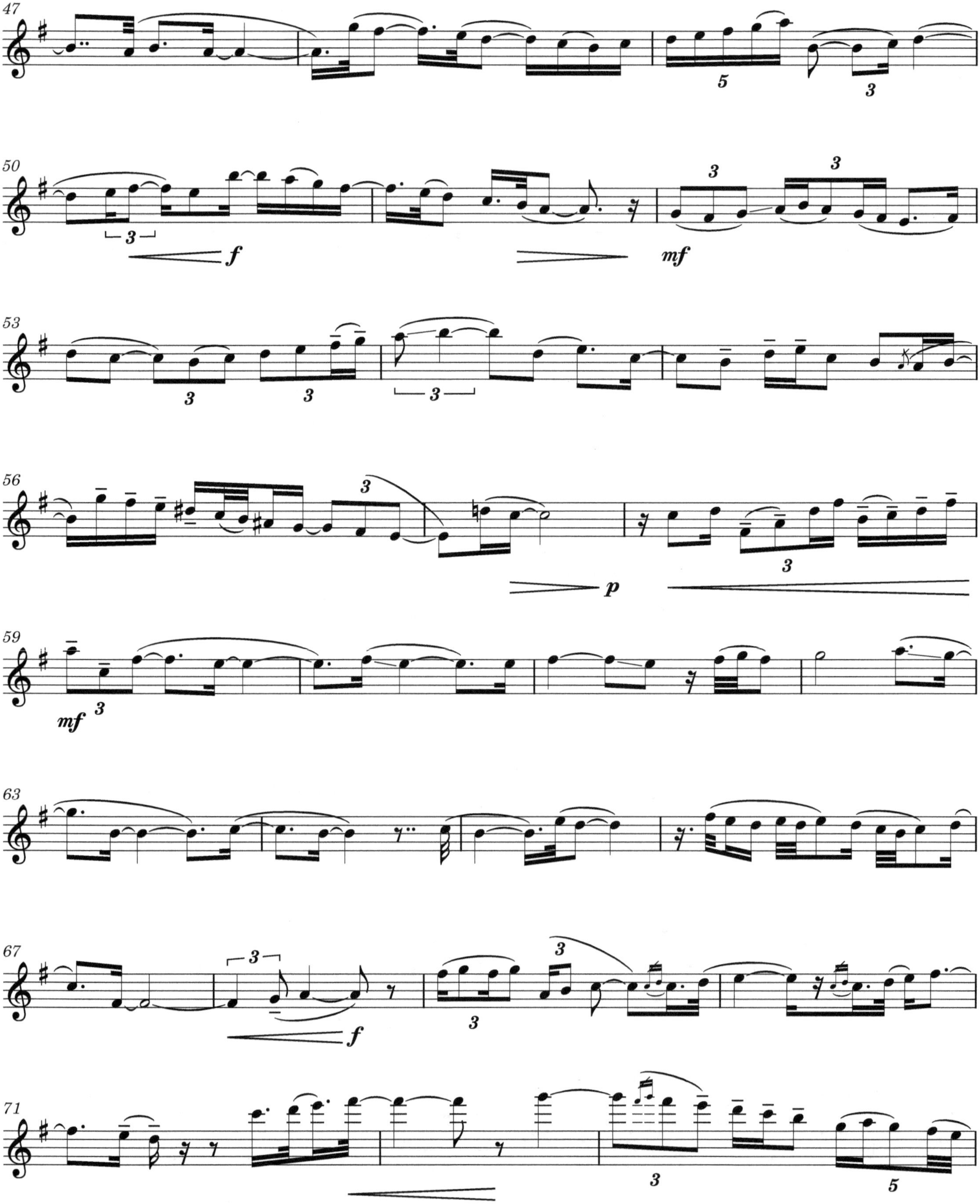
47
50
f
mf
53
56
p
59
mf
63
67
f
71

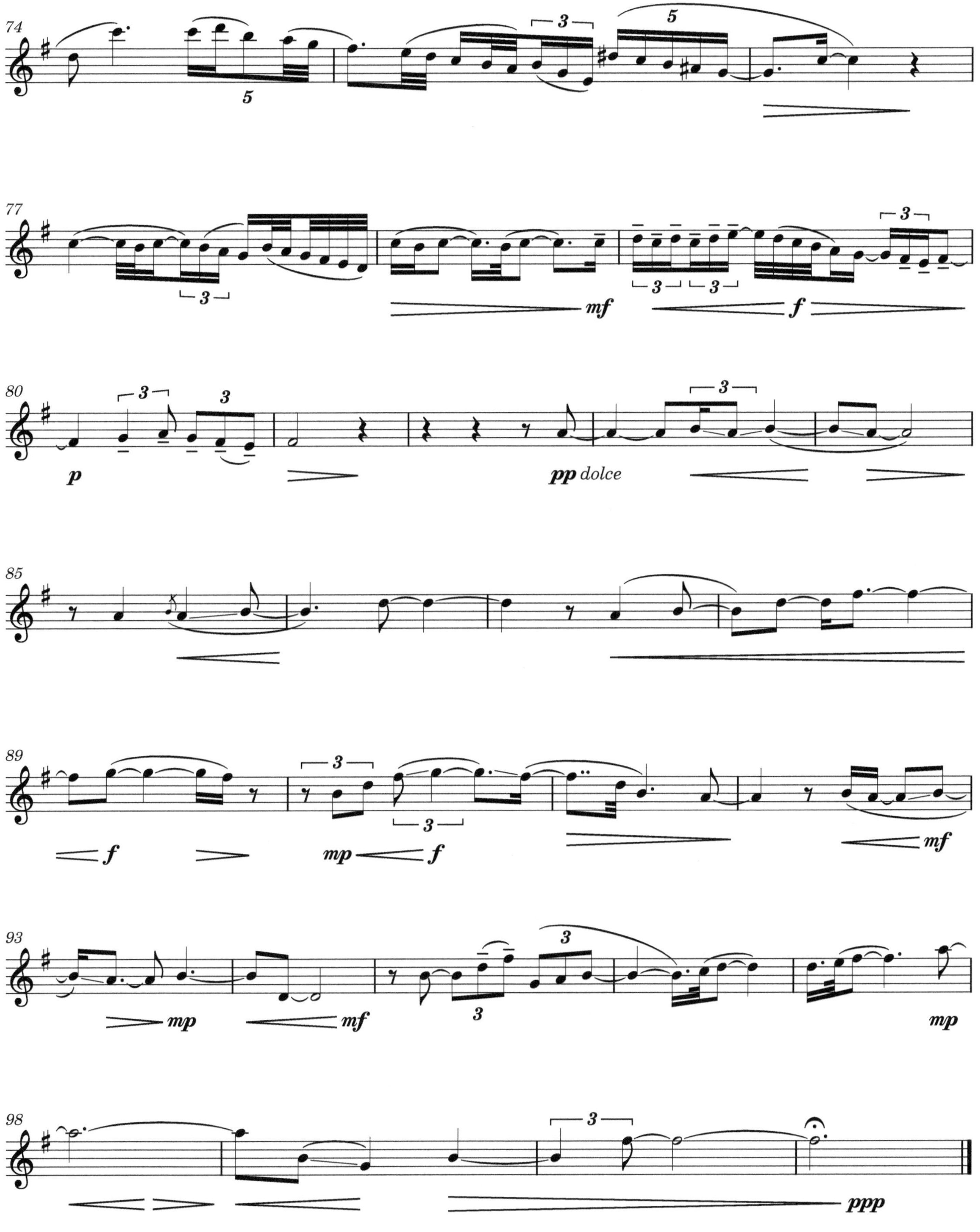
74
77
mf f
80
p
pp dolce
85
89
f
mp f
mf
93
mp
mf
mp
98
ppp

This page intentionally left blank to facilitate page turns

Voix de l'orgue

Saxophone symbols:

Bisbigliando: trille d'une meme jouee avec des doigtes differents
Bisbigliando: tril of the same pitch played with different fingerings
ビスビリャンド：異なる運指による同音のトリル

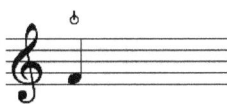

Slap tongue
Slap tongue
スラップ・タンギング

Combinaison de *bisbigliando* et *glissando*
Combination of *bisbigliando* and *glissando*
ビスビリャンドとグリッサンドの組み合わせ

Piano symbols:

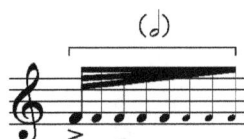

Ralentir depuis rapide a lent librement, avec *diminuendo*, pendant une blanche
Freely *rallentando* from fast to slow, with *diminuendo*, across the duration of a half note
二分音符の間に、ディミヌエンドを伴いながら自由に高速から低速まで減速する

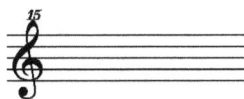

2 octaves plus haut
2 octaves higher
2オクターヴ高く

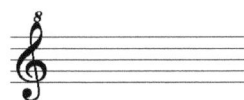

1 octave plus haut
1 octave higher
1オクターヴ高く

à Naomi Shirai

Voix de l'orgue

TETSUYA YAMAMOTO
(2016)

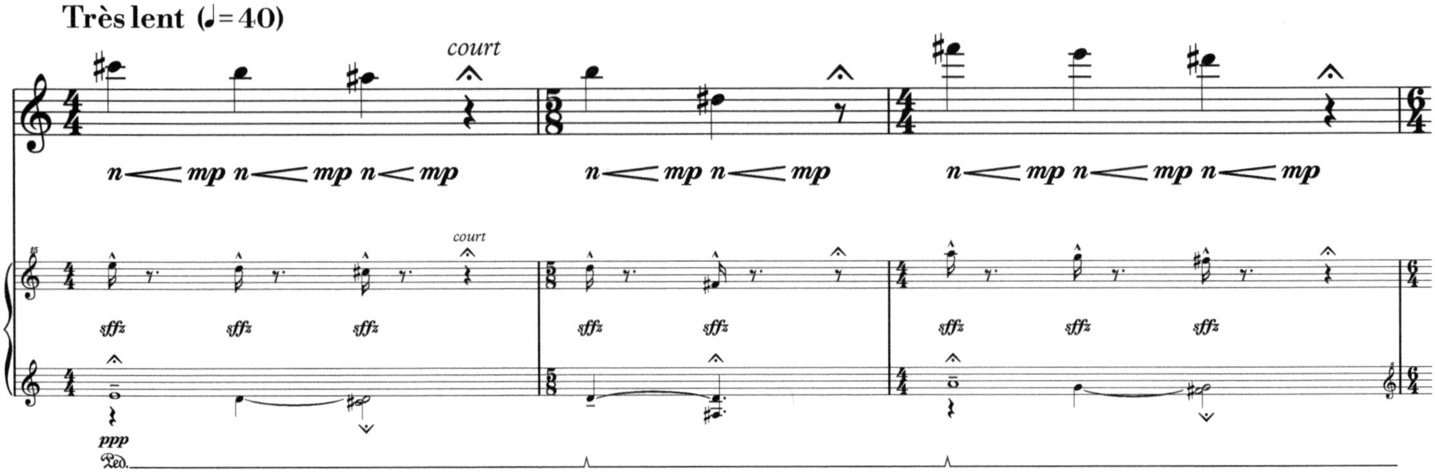

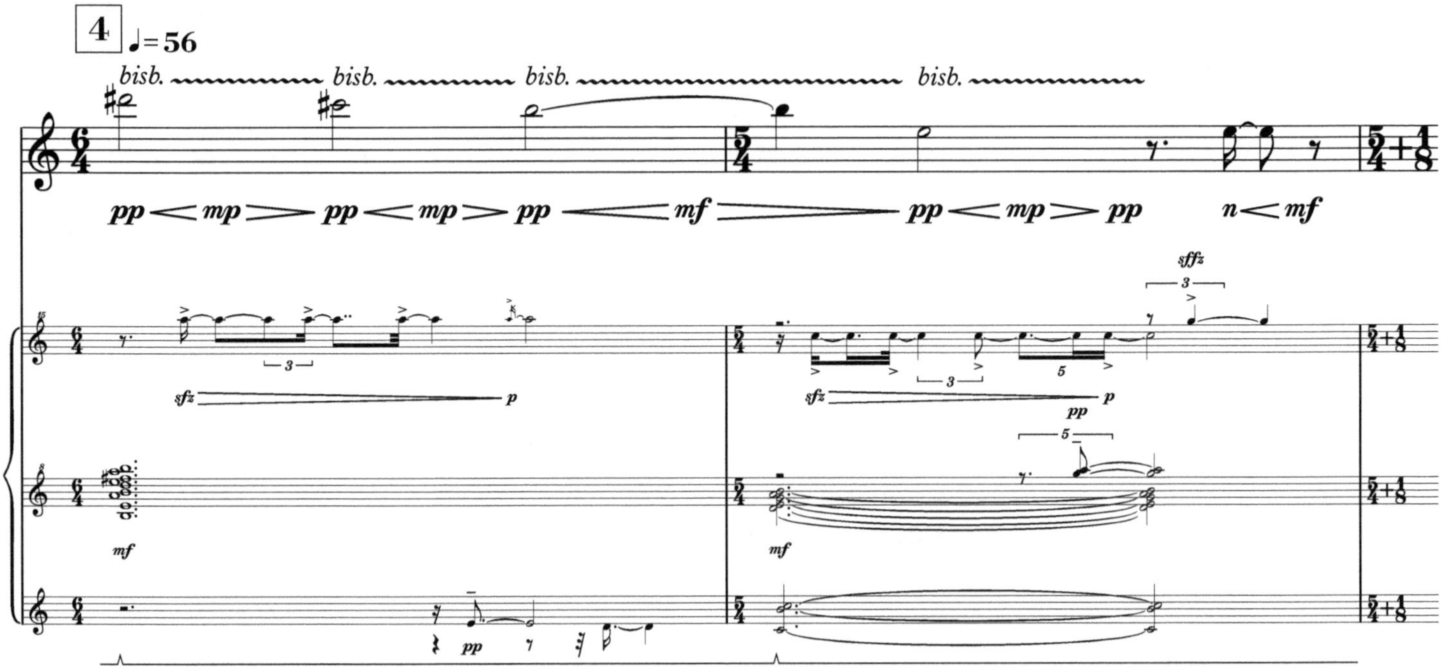

6
bisb.
3
bisb.
slap
bisb.
bisb.
bisb.
pp < mp > pp n < mf pp < mp > pp p pp < mp > pp < mp > pp < mf >
sfz p
pp
5
3
sfz p
mf
mf
3
pp
pp
mpz
pp
8
bisb.
3
bisb.
bisb.
> pp < mp > pp n < mf n < sf pp < mp > pp < mf >
sfz p
5
3
5
3
3
sffz
sffz
sffz
sfz p
mf
pp
3
pp
5
mp
10
bisb.
3
n < p n < p n < p n < p n < sf
mp pp
mp pp
mp pp
mp pp
mp pp

11
bisb.
5
n p n p n p n p n p n sfz
mp pp sfz p
mp mp pp mp pp
mf
(Ped.)
12
bisb.
3 5 3
n mf n mf n mf n mf n mf n mf pp mp pp n
mf pp
5
sfz pp sfz p
mf pp mp
mp p
14
bisb. bisb.
3 5 3
sf n mf n mf n mf n mf pp mp pp mp pp n mf n sf
sfz mf pp mf pp
sfz mp
mf mp
pp mp

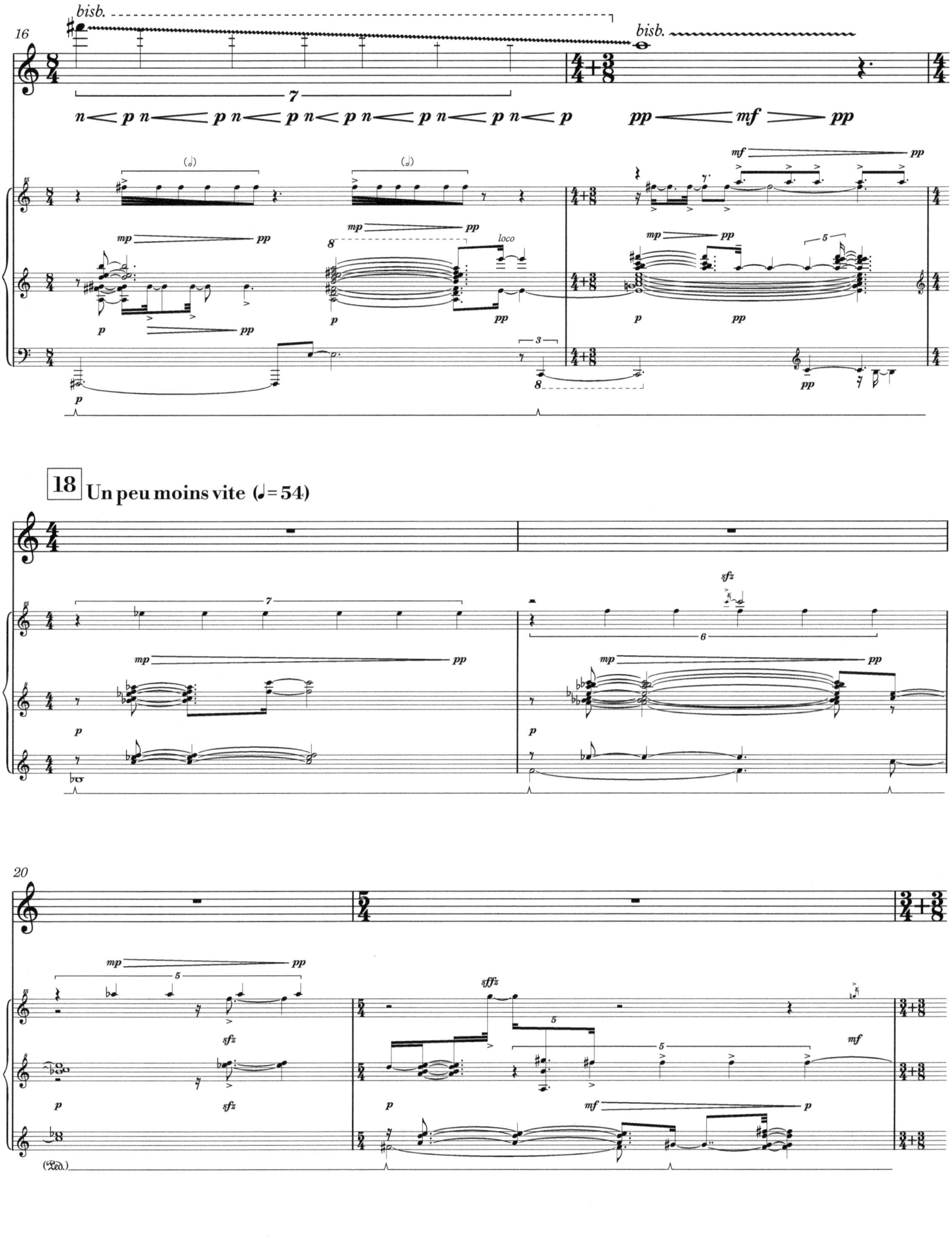
bisb.
bisb.
18 Un peu moins vite (♩=54)
loco
(Ped.)

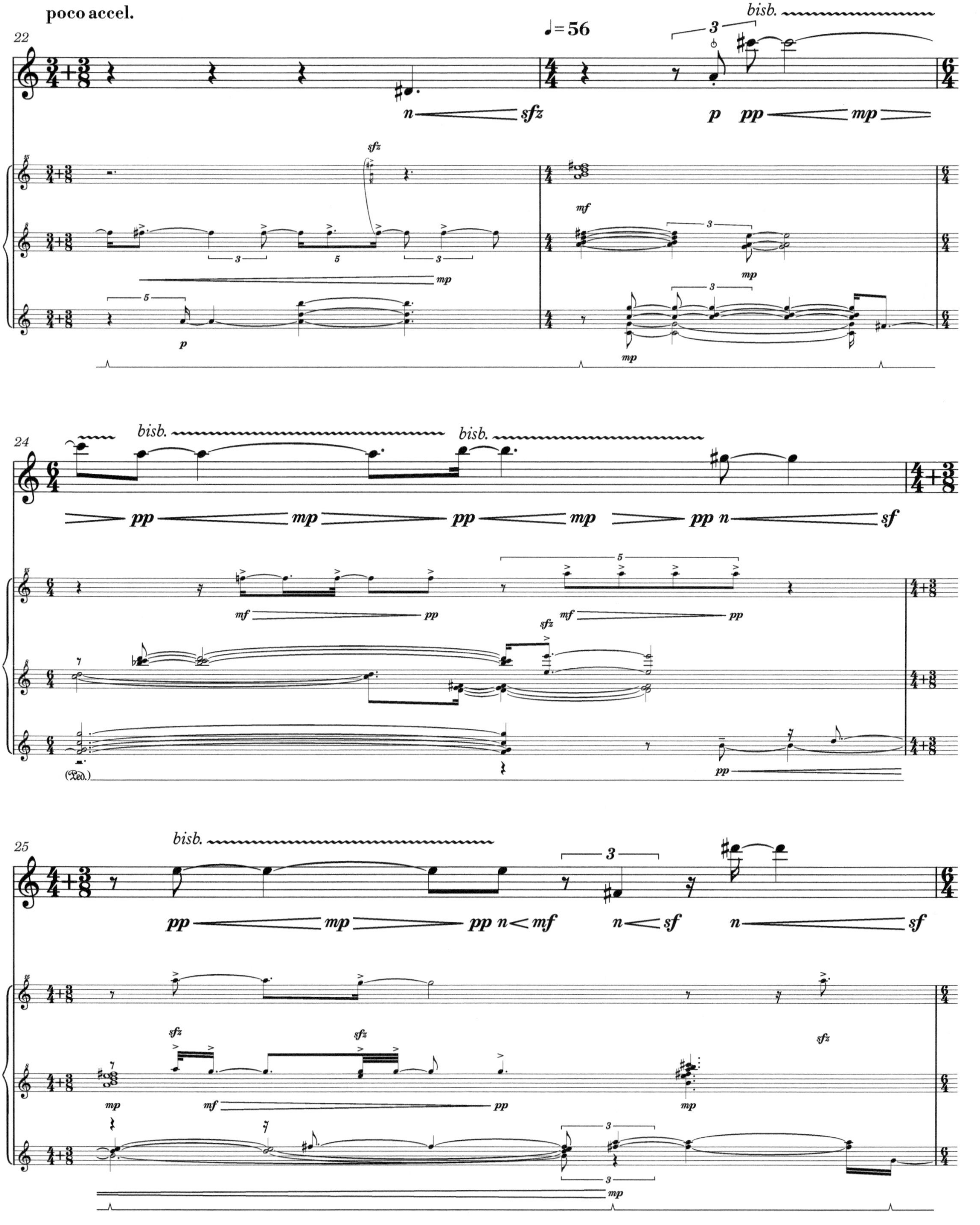
poco accel.
22
♩= 56
bisb.
24
bisb.
bisb.
(Ped.)
25
bisb.

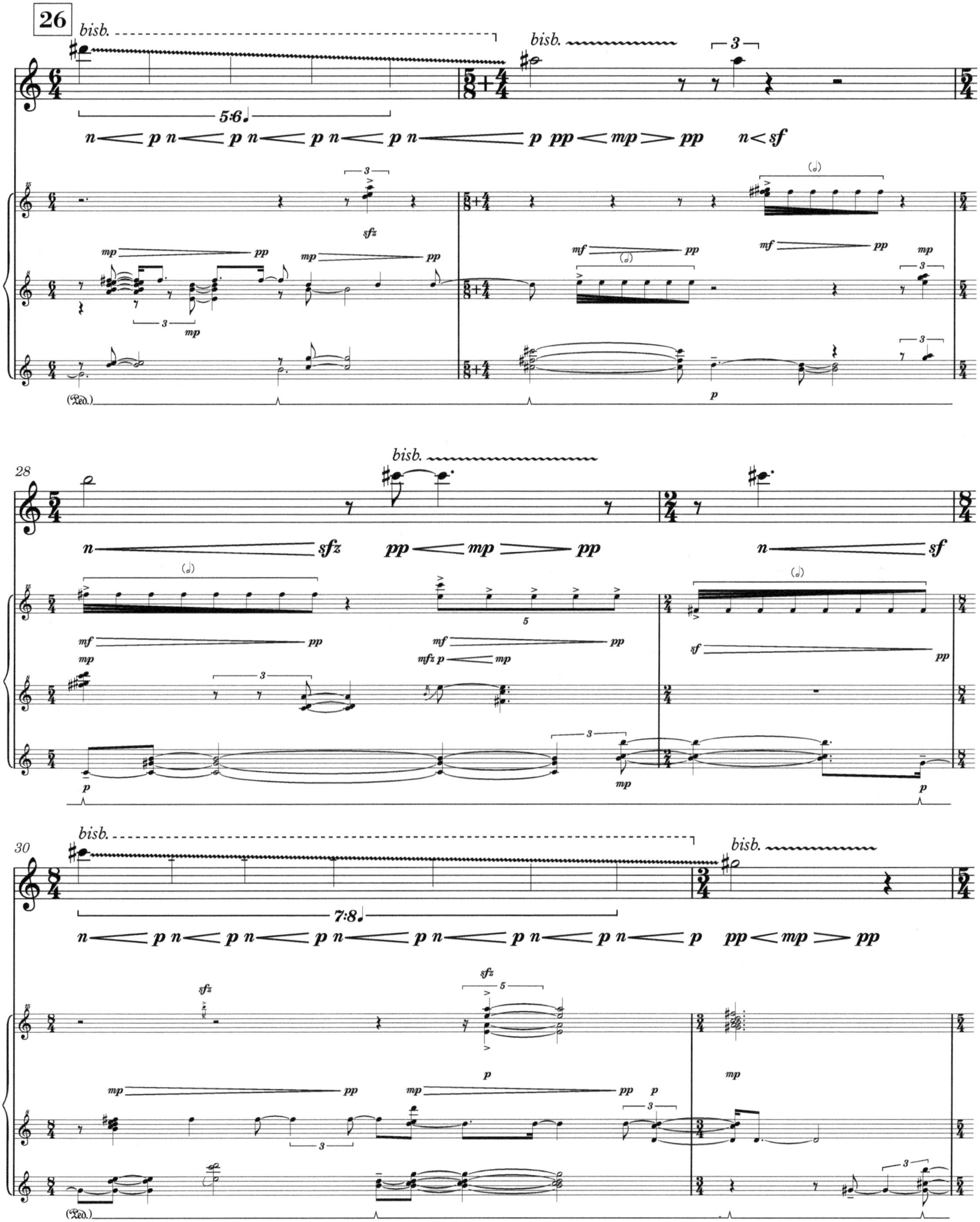
26
bisb.
5:6♩
n < p n < p n < p n < p n < p pp < mp > pp n < sf
(Ped.)
28
bisb.
n < sfz pp < mp > pp n < sf
30
bisb.
7:8♩
n < p n < p n < p n < p n < p n < p n < p pp < mp > pp
(Ped.)

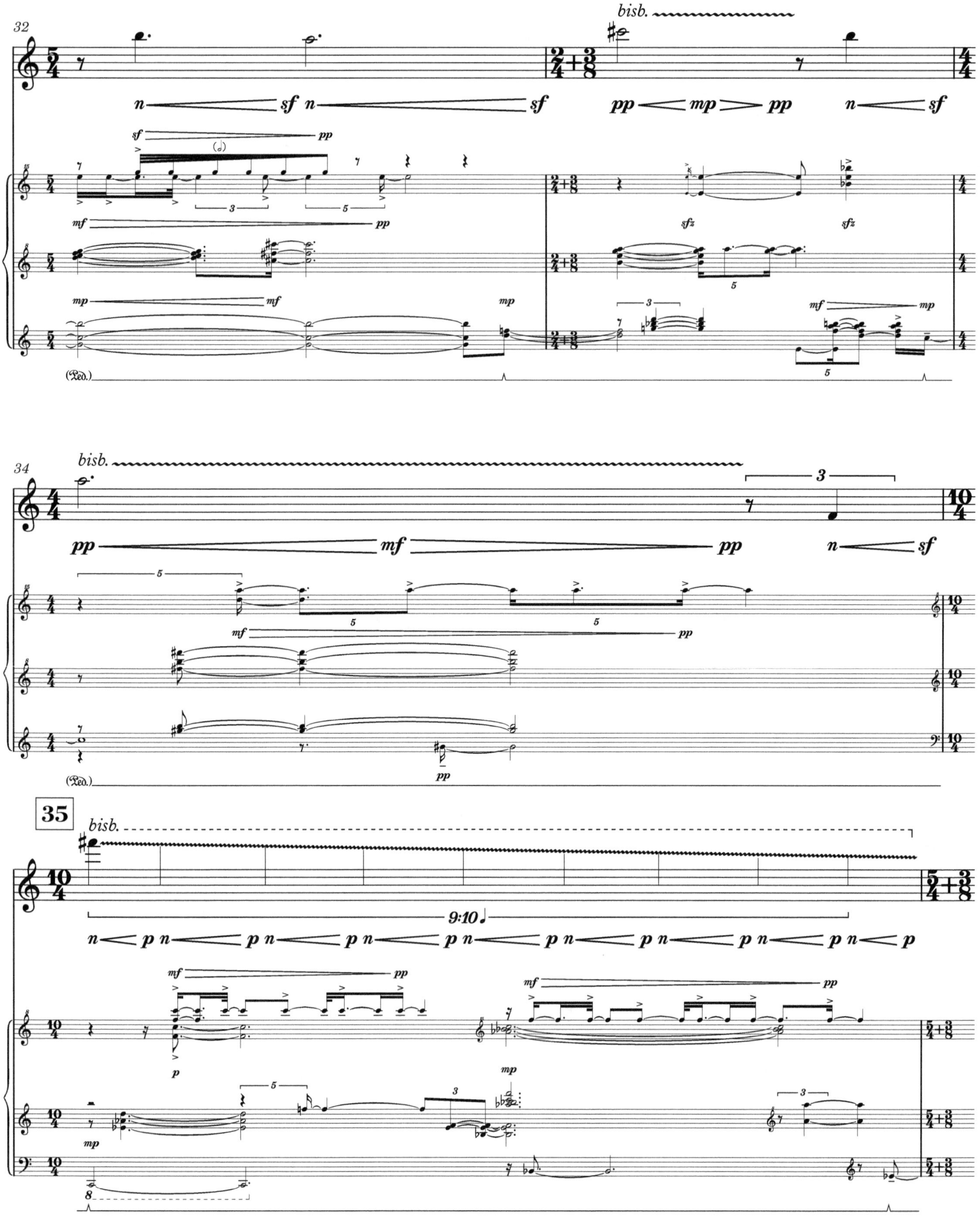
32
bisb.
34
bisb.
35
bisb.
9:10
(Ped.)
(Ped.)

36
bisb. bisb.
pp < mp > pp < mf > pp p n < sf
n < mf n < mf n < mf n < mf n < mf
38
bisb.
pp < mp > pp
n < mf n < sf n < mf n < mf n < mf n < mf
40
bisb.
n < sf pp < mf > pp
p
41
bisb. bisb. bisb.
pp < mp > pp < mp > pp < mp > pp

42
3
bisb.
n mf pp mp pp n sfz
sffz
sffz
sffz
mp
pp
mp
43
bisb.
bisb.
bisb.
pp mp pp mp pp mp pp n mf n mf n mf n mf n
sfz
p
mf
p
p
sfz
p
mp
45
bisb.
bisb.
sfz p pp mf pp n mf pp mf pp
sffz
mf
5
mf
mp
p

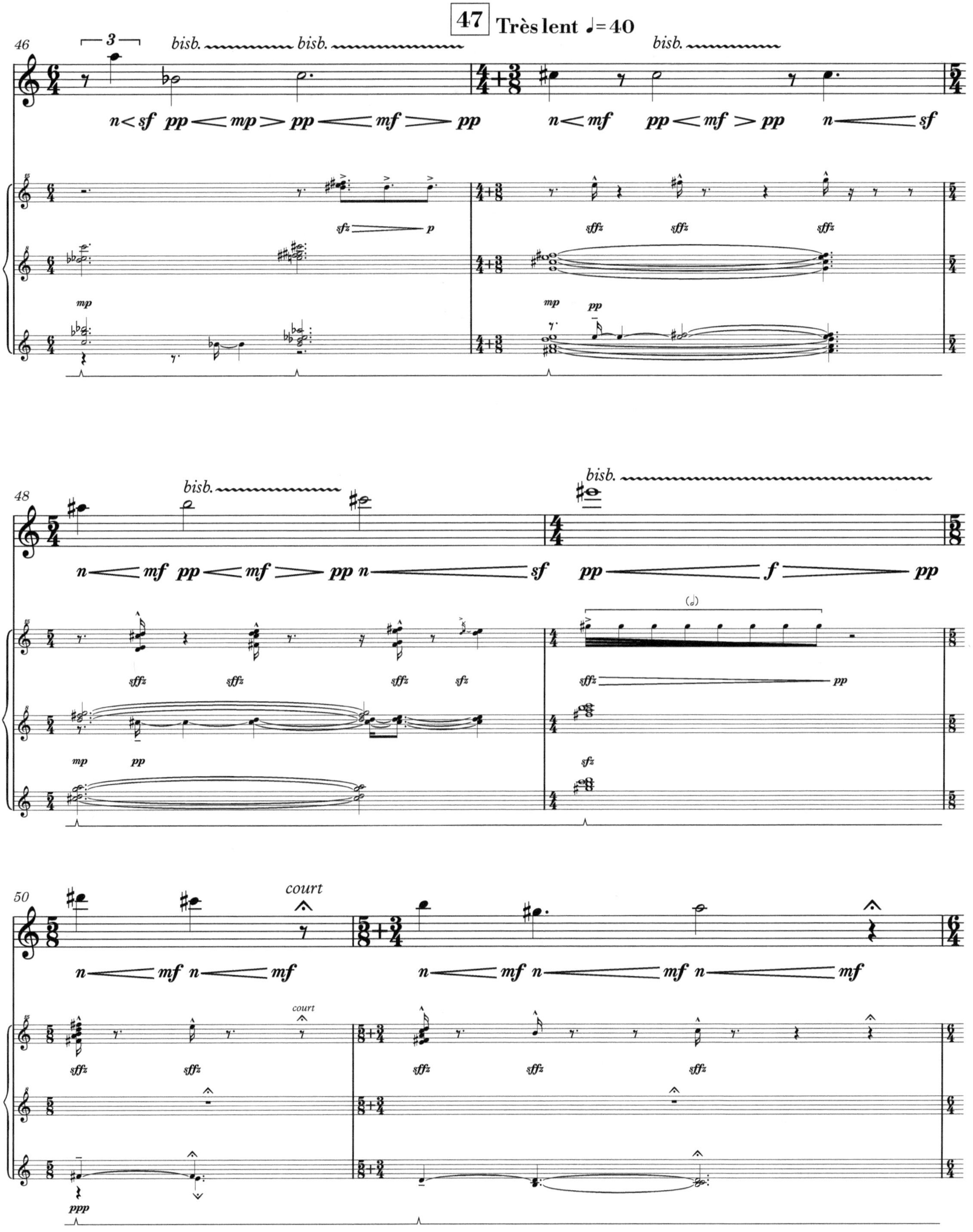
47
Très lent ♩=40
bisb.
bisb.
bisb.
bisb.
bisb.
court
court

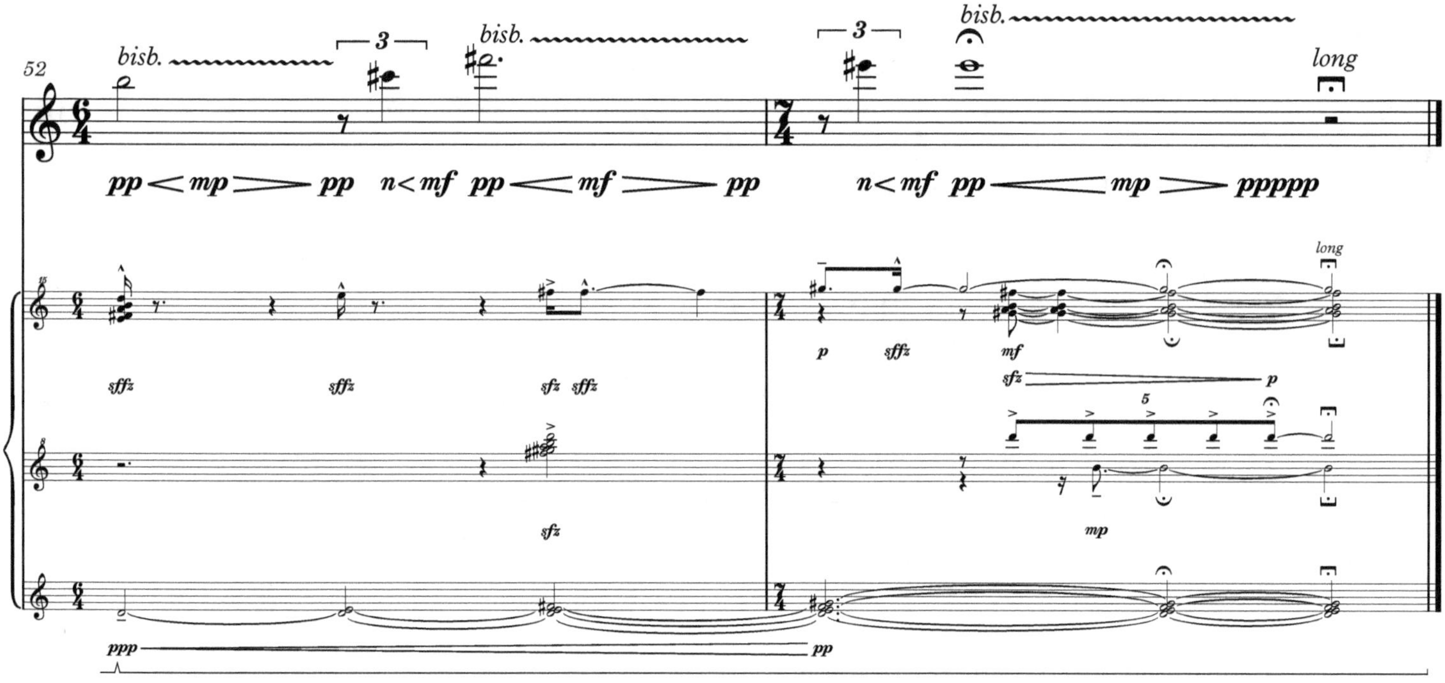
52
bisb.
3
bisb.
3
bisb.
long
pp < mp > pp n < mf pp < mf > pp
n < mf pp < mp > ppppp
long
sffz sffz sfz sffz
p sffz mf
sfz p
5
sfz
mp
ppp pp

This page intentionally left blank to facilitate page turns

Deluge

from Sonata

ROGER ZARE
(2015)

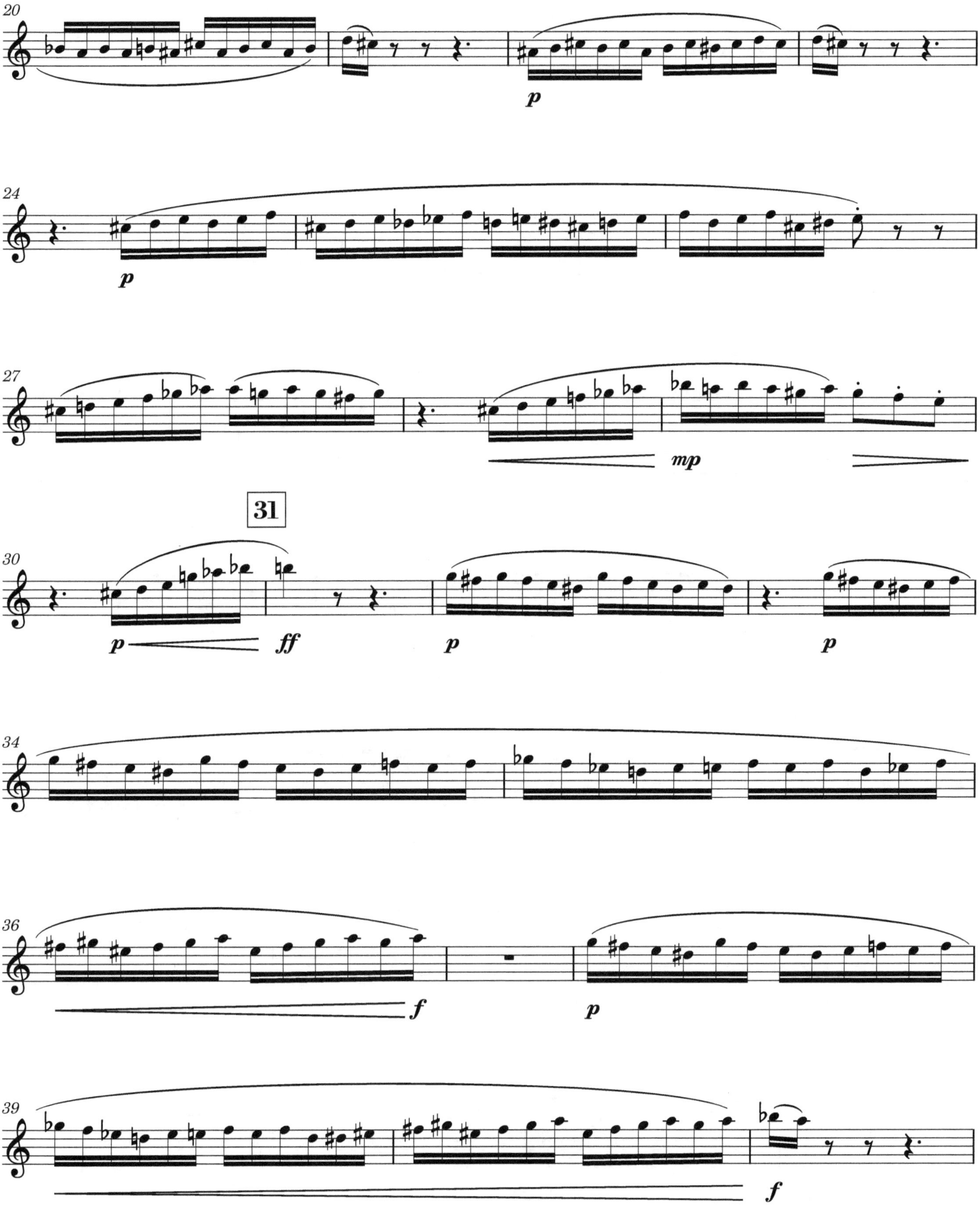
20
p
24
p
27
mp
31
30
p
ff
p
p
34
36
f
p
39
f

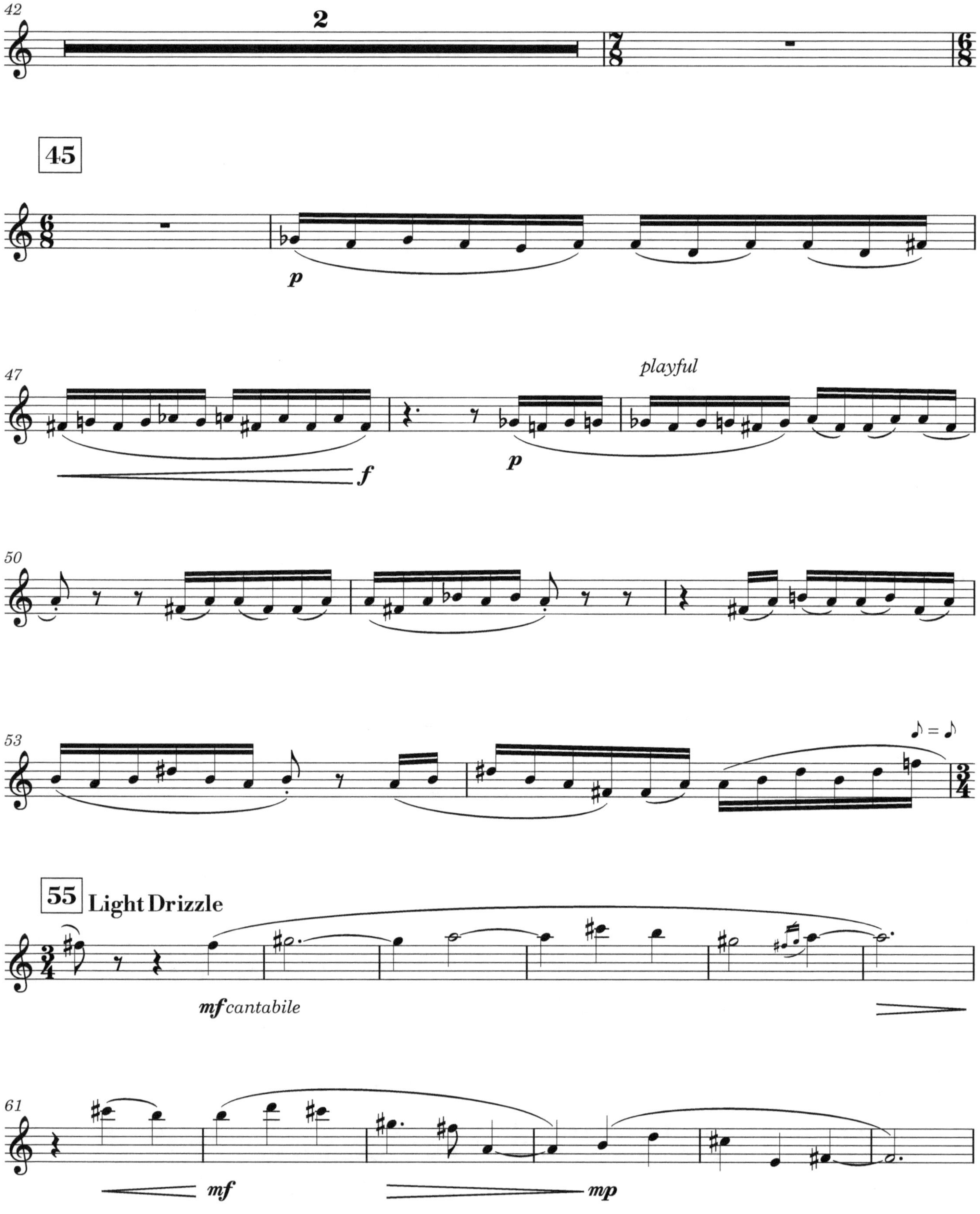
42
2
45
p
47
playful
f
p
50
53
55
Light Drizzle
mf cantabile
61
mf
mp

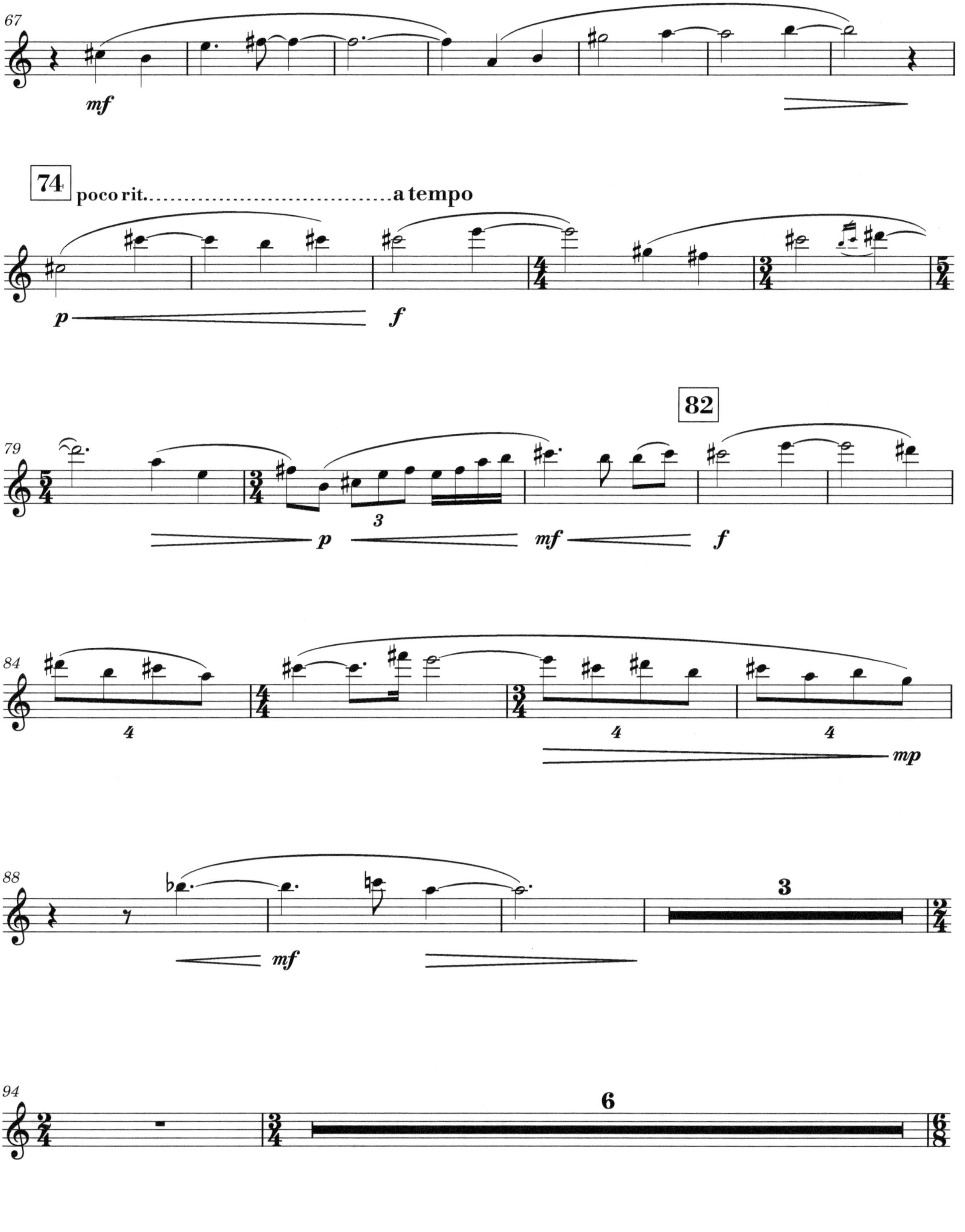
67
mf
74
poco rit. a tempo
p
f
79
82
p
mf
f
84
mp
88
mf
3
94
6

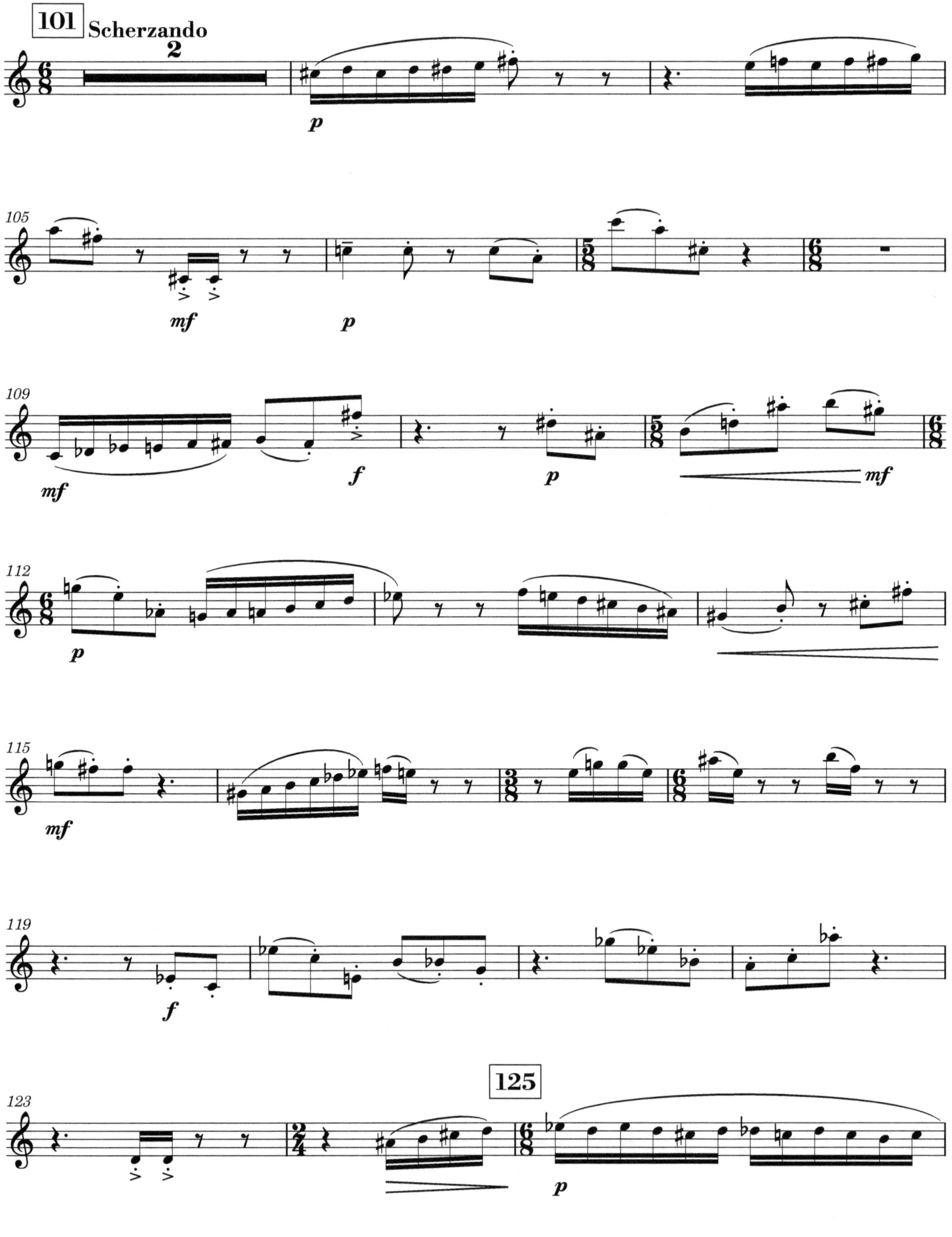
101
Scherzando
2
p
105
mf
p
109
mf
f
p
mf
112
p
115
mf
119
f
123
125
p

126
p
129
mp
p
ff
132
135
p
sffz
p
sffz
ff
140
t.s.
p
sffz
145
f
148
f
151

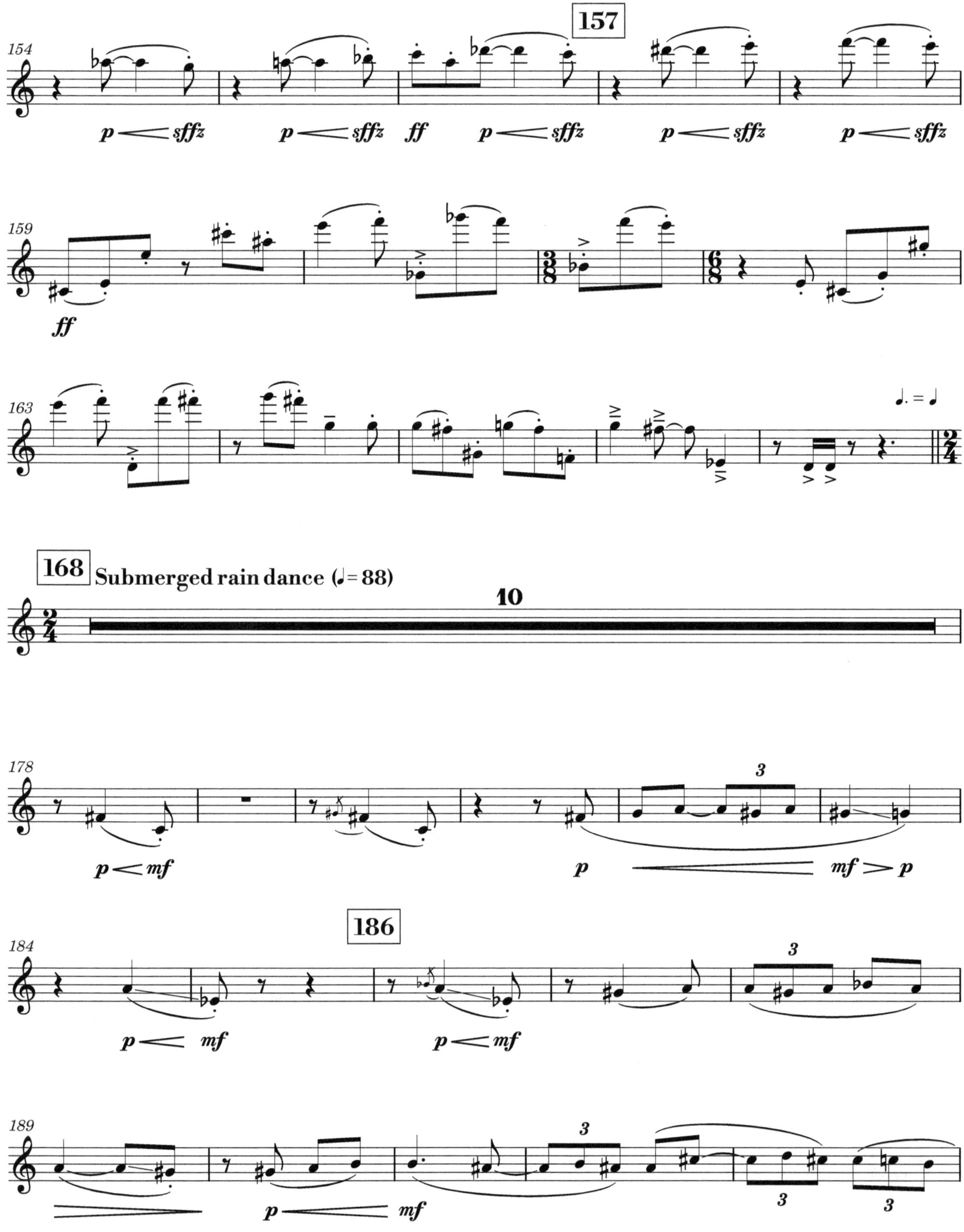
154
157
159
163
168
Submerged rain dance (♩= 88)
10
178
184
186
189

194
p
mf
198
mf
f
p
f
203
p f
p f
t.s.
207
p f
p f
211
p f
p f
ff
fff
216
Tempo I, Downpour (♩=132)
mp cantabile

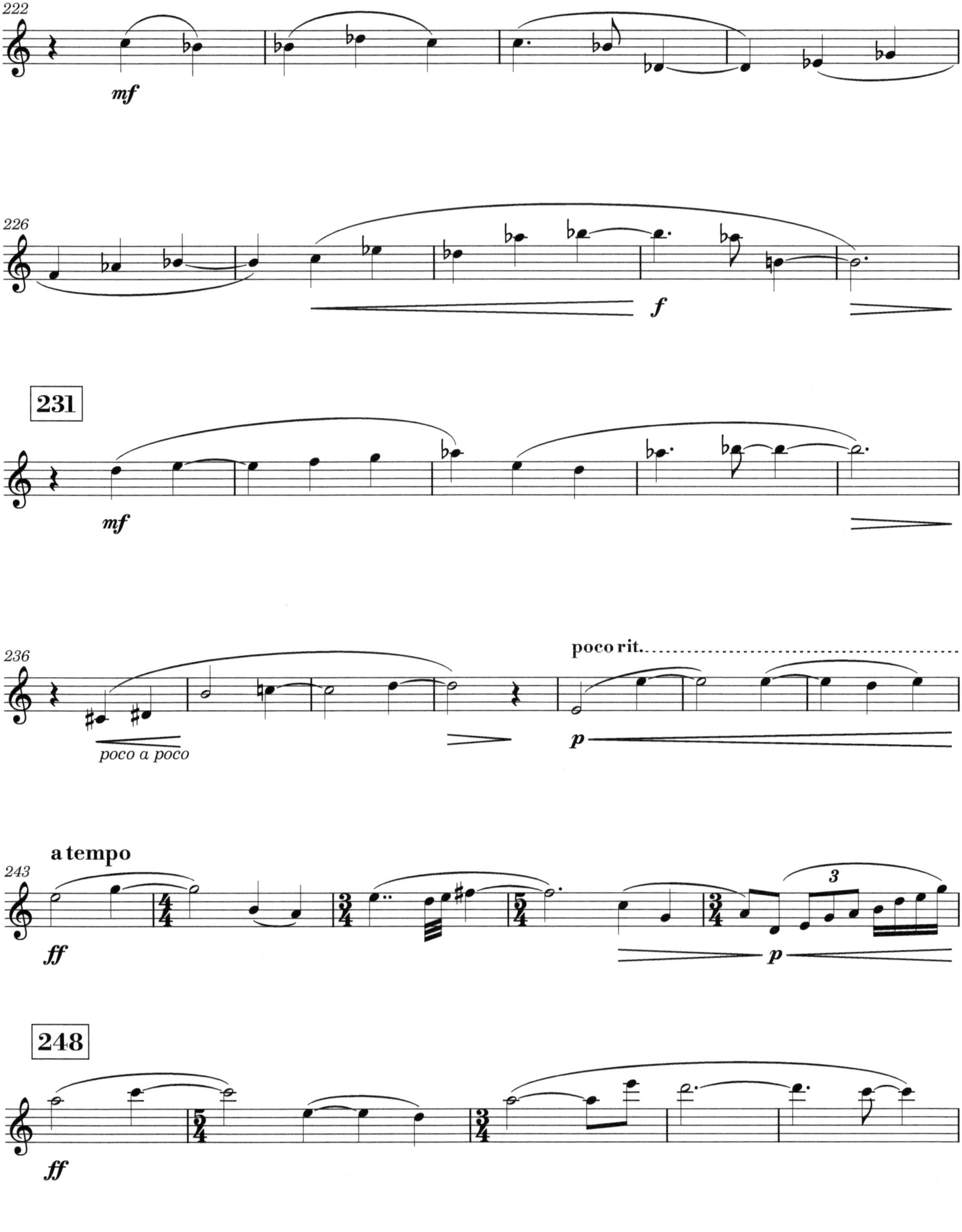
222
mf
226
f
231
mf
236
poco a poco
poco rit.
p
a tempo
243
ff
p
3
248
ff

271 Flash flood

frantic, panicked

82

SUPPLEMENTARY MATERIALS

Texts, program notes, composer biographies, and composer headshots can be found at:

https://newmusicshelf.com/anthologies/alto-sax-v1-info/